CAMBRAI
1917

CAMBRAI
1917

CHRIS MCNAB

First published 2012 by
Spellmount, an imprint of
The History Press
The Mill, Brimscombe Port
Stroud, Gloucestershire, GL5 2QG
www.thehistorypress.co.uk

British Library Cataloguing in Publication Data.
A catalogue record for this book is available from the British Library.

ISBN 978 0 7524 7977 4

Typesetting and origination by The History Press
Manufacturing Managed by Jellyfish Print Solutions Ltd
Printed in Malta by Gutenberg Press.

CONTENTS

ACKNOWLEDGEMENTS

I would like to thank Jo de Vries of The History Press for her professional support and friendship throughout this project, and my family for their forbearance during an unusually busy period of work.

LIST OF ILLUSTRATIONS

1. Tank awaiting the order to advance at Cambrai. *The Illustrated London News*, 1 December 1917.
2. Field Marshal Horatio Herbert Kitchener. *The Illustrated War News*, 1916.
3. Neuve Chapelle and the surrounding advance, captioned in *The Illustrated War News* as 'where the British Army has made a notable advance'. *The Illustrated War News*, 17 March 1915.
4. The infamous 'first day of the Somme' was announced by the explosion of a mine at Hawthorn Ridge on 1 July 1916 at 0730hrs. This day remains one of the bloodiest in the history of the British Army. Photograph taken by Ernest Brooks. Crown Copyright/Public Domain.
5. Sir Douglas Haig.
6. '"Hecatombs" sacrificed to the moloch of Prussian militarism: massed German infantry attacking at Verdun mown down by the French guns.' This version of the attack at Verdun was drawn by Frédéric de Haenen. *The Illustrated War News*, 29 March 1916.
7. The British line as of April 1916. *The Illustrated War News*, 5 April 1916.
8. 'By Hindenburg's orders: "To be held at all costs":

workers) were encouraged to get them to the front as soon as possible. *The Illustrated War News*, 3 May 1916.

21. Soldiers from the Northumberland Fusiliers relax after the Battle of St Eloi. Despite their new steel helmets, they still revel in 'booty' from the enemy – it was common for both sides to collect souvenirs, such as helmets, uniforms, spent cartridges and even weapons. *The Illustrated War News*, 3 May 1916.

22. Here a French artillery bombardment has done it's job on a section of German trench, near Verdun. *The Illustrated War News*, 22 March 1916.

23. A solidly constructed concrete dugout in a captured section of German trench, near Ypres. *The Illustrated War News*, 22 March 1916.

24. British gunner copying gun registrations. *The Book of History, The World's Greatest War*, Vol. XVII, The Grolier Society, New York, 1920. Courtesy of www.gwpda.org.uk

25. German ordnance being moved into position and aligned for firing. *The Illustrated War News*, 12 April 1916.

26. Armoured cars such as these began to prove their worth on the East African front. *The Illustrated War News*, 12 April 1916.

27. An experimental transport tractor van, enabled to move in 'caterpillar fashion' due to the addition of tracks. Such vehicles as these were a precusor to the tank. *The Illustrated War News*, 19 April 1916.

28. The tank made famous by the Battle of Cambrai. This iconic image has come to represent the birth of tank warfare during the First World War. *The Illustrated London News*, 1 December 1917.

29. 'Crusty' crosses a shell-hole, although many tanks were to get bogged down in such obstacles during the battle. *The Illustrated London News*, 1 December 1917.

30. A French fire trench at Verdun. *The Illustrated War News*, 26 April 1916.

31. Map showing the British line before the advance and the

deep German fire trench. *The Illustrated London News*, 1 December 1917.

46. A Highlander bringing in two captured German machine-gunners. *The Illustrated London News*, 1 December 1917.

47. Irish troops rest alongside northern county units and the Scottish Territorials. *The Illustrated London News*, 1 December 1917.

48. Irish troops in action, crossing the German second line. *The Illustrated London News*, 1 December 1917.

49. German prisoners are used as stretcher-bearers, carrying a wounded British officer to a first aid post. *The Illustrated London News*, 1 December 1917.

50. The evolution in aeroplane technology was continual throughout the Great War, as the RFC played an increasingly important role in Allied operations. Here a new double-engined biplane with central gun is being inspected. *The Illustrated War News*, 31 May 1916.

51. Captured German field guns waiting to be removed by British troops, near Ribécourt. *The Illustrated London News*, 1 December 1917.

52. Despite both the British and Germans claiming success, both sides still felt the pain of heavy casualties after Cambrai. *The Illustrated London News*, 1 December 1917.

53. Villagers are evacuated from Noyelles, escaping the heavy German machine-gun fire. *The Illustrated London News*, 1 December 1917.

54. Tanks often found it difficult and dangerous to manouevre through narrow village streets. *The Illustrated London News*, 1 December 1917.

55. Cavalry slowly wend their way over a reserve line road in territory just captured from the Germans. *The Illustrated London News*, 1 December 1917.

56. After Cambrai, the British government were keen to extol the virtues of the tank to the public. Here, one of the tanks used in the Cambrai battle is placed in Trafalgar Square as a 'tank bank', encouraging visitors to purchase a 'tank bond'

INTRODUCTION

On 23 November 1917, church bells rang out across London, tolled in jubilation at what appeared to be a great British victory unfolding across the English Channel in northern France. The First World War had by now been convulsing Europe since August 1914. For three long years, the British Army had launched periodic offensives on the Western Front, each carrying with it hopes of punching through the formidable German trench lines and bringing about a general collapse of the Kaiser's army. The names associated with these offensives have become part of the British historical psyche – Neuve Chapelle, Arras, Somme, Ypres (Passchendaele) – yet, instead of bringing about German defeat, these blood-soaked attacks famously purchased massive British and Commonwealth casualties for extremely limited gains. Most notoriously, the first day of the Battle of the Somme (1 July 1916) resulted in 57,470 British casualties, including 19,240 dead. The battle would drag on until the winter of 1916, taking the British casualty count up beyond 600,000 for a maximum depth of advance of just 6 miles.

The attack at Cambrai – launched on 20 November 1917 – appeared to be different. Tactically and technologically it was more sophisticated, particularly in the use of artillery and the armour of the nascent Tank Corps. The attack was launched with the benefit of surprise, achieved through painstaking night-time deployments of guns, tanks and men, and the avoidance of an extensive preparatory bombardment (the traditional signal of an impending infantry assault). Pre-offensive intelligence had been used comprehensively, building up a detailed picture of the forces and positions opposite.

The preparation seemed to pay off. The British drove forward nearly 4 miles in just a few hours on that chilly, overcast November morning, an unprecedented physical surge that lifted the hearts of the British people and caused the bells to peal out in joy. The German Hindenburg Line defences appeared to be mortally wounded, and the British and Commonwealth journalists wrote with a confident satisfaction as they viewed events unfolding. The *Daily Mail* proclaimed the offensive a 'Splendid Success', and one New Zealand journalist stated that:

> Sir Douglas Haig's great and splendidly successful stroke in the region between St. Quentin and the Scarpe is one of the surprises of the war … The ingeniously conceived and well executed coup which has driven the Germans back over so considerable a distance is bound to have far-reaching effects.
>
> *Marlborough Express*, 24 November 1917

Optimism is a fragile gift in war, and the bells and eulogies of those late days of November did indeed prove to be premature. The German forces around Cambrai flexed, recovered, then counter-attacked, and with brutal commitment began to claw back many of the gains made by the British. By the end of the first week of December the British push had collapsed, with another 44,000 casualties added to the lists. An offensive born in victory withered into stalemate and wearying disappointment.

As we shall see in this book, Cambrai was a battle in which old and new ways of warfare were still imperfectly merging. The old ways were represented by the 'poor bloody infantry' – overburdened, tired and armed with rifle and bayonet – and the cavalry, a relic of a former age that was desperately attempting to justify its existence. The new ways of war were the tools of mechanised slaughter: machine-guns (both light and heavy), poison gas, combat aircraft, long-range artillery and tanks. Battlefield communications, the glue that could provide co-operation between these elements, were still haphazard and could be severed in the microseconds it took for a shell-burst to slash through a field telephone cable. The friction between traditional human warriors and machines capable of mass killing power produced the dizzying death tolls of many First World War battles.

Subsequent histories of the First World War, particularly those that followed during the revisionist and less patriotic 1960s and '70s, put much of the blame for nearly 1 million British dead firmly on the shoulders of the commanders, the infantry themselves classically portrayed as 'lions led by donkeys'. This view was cemented by accounts such as Alan Clark's *The Donkeys* (1961), and in more recent times it was popularly evoked by plays such as *Oh What a Lovely War!* and TV dramas like Ben Elton and Richard Curtis' *Blackadder Goes Forth*. In the latter, Stephen Fry's immaculately portrayed General Melchett, supported by his sycophantic aide Captain Darling, blithely consigns his men to death in battle for little purpose and with no compunction. Rowan Atkinson's Captain Blackadder, with infinite weariness, declares that Haig's next 'big push' is nothing more than 'another gargantuan effort to move his drinks cabinet six inches closer to Berlin'.

Thankfully, much current research has shown that the real command picture of the First World War is far more nuanced and complex. Richard Holmes in *Tommy* rightly points out that British commanders were no strangers to death and danger – fifty-eight generals were killed during the war and 'Three divisional commanders were killed at Loos in September 1915, more British divisional commanders than were killed by enemy fire in the whole of the Second World War' (Richard Holmes, *Tommy*, Harperperennial, 2005, p.xx).

Holmes and others, such as Gary Sheffield (see his *Forgotten Victory*), have also shown that what we might see as the tactics of unimaginative slaughter are more understandable when we genuinely engage with the actual command conditions of the time. The British commanders went from leading small expeditionary operations in far-flung corners of the British Empire to managing tens of thousands of men in industrial combat on the Western Front and elsewhere. Their negotiation of this new world was hampered tactically by the poor state of battlefield communications, which often meant that once a fight was under way it was almost impossible to make nimble, real-time modifications to the battle plan. Tactics were therefore often simplistic and operational objectives frequently broad. Such is not to deny that the First World War was graced with its share of incompetent or over-promoted commanders, but this is true of all wars.

The burdens of command in the First World War must be borne in mind as we study the Battle of Cambrai. Equally, we must also acknowledge that there were innovators in the British Army, men who sought to adapt warfare to new technological and tactical possibilities. For what seems undeniable is that the Battle of Cambrai does at least represent the imperfect attempt to embrace a new form of combined-arms warfare, in which armour, infantry, aircraft, artillery and intelligence worked co-operatively to achieve more decisive battlefield results. Taking lessons from the failures and experiments of previous engagements, officers such as General Sir Julian Byng, Brigadier General Hugh Elles, Lieutenant Colonel John Fuller, Major General John Davidson and even the British commander-in-chief, Sir Douglas Haig, pursued or permitted fresh tactical approaches at Cambrai, and the greatest use of tanks since they were first introduced on to the Somme in 1916. Hence, despite the fact that the British *Official History* of Cambrai concluded that the offensive 'showed little profit', the battle captures our imagination today as a precursor of mobile warfare, an augur of the rolling armoured engagements of France in 1940 or of North Africa in 1942.

1. Tank awaiting the order to advance at Cambrai. The Illustrated London News, 1 December 1917.

Yet caution is also required here, particularly regarding the role of armour. Cambrai has been popularly labelled history's 'first tank battle', primarily on account of the unprecedented volume of armour committed to the campaign (476 tanks were assembled for the attack, 350 of those being combat vehicles) and its central role in the advances of the first hours of the campaign. Some post-war analysts, including the great Sir Winston Churchill, even went so far as to claim that had the technology and tactics of Cambrai been applied to the offensives of 1915–17, the war might have developed very differently. (Admittedly, Churchill had an eye to posterity here, as a former head of the Landships Committee that pioneered the development of tanks from 1915.)

Although there is an element of truth in Churchill's views, there is also much hyperbole. As this book will show, the value of the tank on the Cambrai battlefield can and has been overstated. Some 180 British tanks were out of action by the end of the first day of a campaign that ran for nearly three weeks. The Germans were initially routed as much by the sheer surprise of the offensive as by the appearance of massed armour, and they quickly recovered. Moreover, the presence of tanks must not mask the fact that Cambrai was a major infantry engagement, one that cost a combined 90,000 casualties on both sides. Even if we grant Cambrai as the 'first tank battle', we must never fall into the trap of discussing it as *purely* a tank battle, with the infantry and cavalry in a secondary role.

The other oft-neglected element in many histories of Cambrai is the skill and innovation of the German counter-attacks that reversed the British gains. These counter-attacks were delivered with as much aplomb as the British offensive itself, and they displayed some elements of the *Stoßtruppen* ('shock troops' or, more popularly, 'storm troopers') tactics that would be applied to even greater effect in the German offensives of 1918. Giving more weight to the British efforts at Cambrai is understandable for British historians, eager to explore the nation's martial history, but it is only part of the story.

Ultimately, the Battle of Cambrai is a human narrative, like all battles. For the individual soldier who took part, the offensive was about the portion of field or woodland in front of him, the comrade by his side and the demands of surviving until the end of the day. The picture 'on the ground' can be very different, therefore, to the picture from the historian's overview, but ultimately I shall attempt to do justice to both.

TIMELINE

1914

3–4 August	Germany declares war on France and Belgium, invading Belgium on 3 August
5–10 September	German invasion of France stopped at the First Battle of the Marne
September–December	German, British and French forces establish trench networks running from the Channel coast down to Switzerland

1915

10–13 March	Failed British offensive at Neuve Chapelle
22 April–25 May	Second Battle of Ypres; German forces use poison gas
25 September–14 October	First Battle of Loos. Major British offensive that includes British use of poison gas and of the 'creeping' artillery barrage. Costs 50,000 British casualties
19 December	Douglas Haig becomes commander-in-chief of the British Expeditionary Force (BEF)

1916

21 February–18 December	The Germans force the French into a massive battle of attrition around Verdun. The campaign eventually costs the Germans as many casualties as the French, and by December the German forces have lost all their initial gains

Timeline

1916	**1 July–18 November**	The Battle of the Somme. This major British offensive is launched to relieve pressure on the French at Verdun. For limited gains the British suffer more than 600,000 casualties. Tanks used for first time in combat
1917	**February**	German forces on the Western Front, weakened by fighting in 1916, are forced to withdraw back to the Hindenburg Line
	6 April	The United States declares war on Germany
	April–May	A British offensive at Arras and French attack at Chemin des Dames both end with few solid results, except thousands of casualties
	31 July–10 November	Third Battle of Ypres. A major British offensive runs aground in appalling weather and in the face of terrible casualties – 400,000 men are killed or wounded. Germans take similar punishment, however
	13 October	Operation GY receives approval from Haig
	20 November	Operation GY is launched, making impressive first-day gains through the Hindenburg Line
	21 November	The offensive continues with British assaults on Bourlon, Fontaine and Cantaing, plus crossings of the St Quentin canal
	23–27 November	There is intensive fighting across the Cambrai front, particularly around Bourlon and Fontaine, but the British advance has effectively stalled
	30 November	A heavily reinforced German Second Army begins a major counter-attack at Cambrai, pushing back British forces in the south but making little headway in the north

1917

4–7 December   The British make a phased withdrawal back to the Flesquières Ridge Line. At this point both sides stop major offensive operations and the Battle of Cambrai is over

HISTORICAL BACKGROUND

By December 1914, the Western Front had etched into stalemate in the fields of France and Belgium. The German plan for a quick victory over France – a modified version of a plan developed by Chief of Staff Alfred von Schlieffen in 1905 – failed in realisation, defeated by logistical problems, unexpectedly tough British and French resistance and a rapid Russian mobilisation in the East. Instead, while the Eastern Front would continue to be characterised by physically dynamic campaigns, in the West the two sides faced each other from static trench positions that stretched from the North Sea to the Swiss border.

For the British, the early months of the war brought numerous profound challenges. First and foremost was the need for mobilisation. At the onset of war, Britain had a regular army of just under 250,000 men, plus a reserve of about 270,000 part-time Territorial soldiers. The British Expeditionary Force (BEF) deployed to France and Belgium was initially only six infantry divisions and one cavalry division strong (about 150,000 men). These soldiers gave a good account of themselves, but the German Army in 1914 had a total standing army manpower of 900,000, plus more than 2 million reservists. Even with 700,000 French troops by their side, it was clear that the British were outnumbered.

2. Field Marshal Horatio Herbert Kitchener. The Illustrated War News, 1916.

The problem was solved by one of the most impressive military recruitment campaigns in history, pioneered by the Secretary of State for War, Field Marshal Horatio Kitchener. Within days of launching the appeal for volunteers, some 500,000 more men had joined the ranks of 'Kitchener's Armies', and by the end of 1915 just under 2.5 million volunteers had enlisted.

The Offensives of 1915

With additional manpower at the front, the British sought aggressive opportunities in 1915, the army's high command becoming frustrated with the emerging possibility of a prolonged conflict. On 10 March 1915, Sir Douglas Haig's First Army pushed forward at Neuve Chapelle in Artois, the BEF commander-in-chief, Sir John French, having argued for a more offensive spirit amongst British forces. (The attack was meant to be part of wider operations, but troop diversions to Ypres and the Allied operation in the Dardanelles reduced the offensive to a localised action.) After a thirty-five-minute bombardment from 342 guns, the infantry went on the attack and quickly took the village of Neuve Chapelle, a key objective. Then, however, the momentum bled out of the attack. The lack of real-time combat communications proved to be an acute problem, and artillery support dwindled. As a result the offensive had petered out by 13 March, with the primary objective of Aubers lying beyond reach.

The failure of Neuve Chapelle brought public recriminations in Britain, and yet it did not dampen the desire for further offensives. Indeed, 1915 was a year of regular French, British and German attacks, giving the Western Front lots of light, thunder and blood but little in the way of physical change. The French launched themselves against the St Mihiel salient on 5 April, then more broadly in Artois and Vimy Ridge in May, and Champagne in September. The Germans, in their only major offensive of the year, attempted to cut out the vital British salient at Ypres in Belgium on 22 April, beginning a month-long campaign that was made infamous by the widespread use of poison gas (in this case, chlorine gas) amongst the German opening moves. On the part of the British (which in this book will also be shorthand for Commonwealth forces), Haig's men supported the French in the Artois offensive in May, attacking Festubert on the 15th. Then on 25 September, six divisions of British troops pushed out

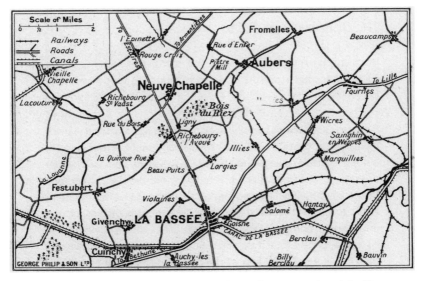

3. Neuve Chapelle and the surrounding advance, captioned in The Illustrated War News as 'where the British Army has made a notable advance'. The Illustrated War News, 17 March 1915.

against the German lines at Loos in the Pas-de-Calais. This battle ran until 14 October, and although the British were able to make some moderate gains – including the capture of Loos itself – the offensive eventually ground to a halt with 50,000 casualties.

What is remarkable about the campaigns of 1915 is how so much energy was expended for so little physical gain. A common theme developed. When launched, attacks tended to meet with initial, localised successes, but within a few days the advances ran out of steam, blunted on a strengthening enemy defence as the enemy pushed in reinforcements or even made a counter-attack, and on account of problems bringing up reserve forces to support the push.

The experience of 1915 also threw a spotlight on how much warfare had changed since the end of the nineteenth century. Trench warfare itself may have had a primitive, troglodyte element

THE BATTLE OF LOOS

At the Battle of Loos the British made advances of 4,000yds, captured Loos and took over a 4-mile section of German frontline defences, all in the first few hours. On the second day, by contrast, the Germans had strengthened its defence along its second line with horrendous results – machine-gunners massacred about 6,000 British soldiers in just two days, the Germans eventually re-labelling the area the 'Field of Corpses of Loos'.

underpinning it, but there was nothing primitive about the new weaponry that was being deployed. Tightly packed ranks of infantry advancing slowly over open ground might have been appropriate during the Napoleonic era, but by the First World War such tactics were little short of suicidal. Artillery, machine-guns and efficient bolt-action rifles meant that entire expanses of ground could be turned into lethal 'beaten zones'. Furthermore, extensive defensive systems such as barbed wire and minefields could either slow an attack or channel it into ground of the defenders' choosing – either option could bring the attackers directly under the mouths of waiting and pre-ranged guns. In these conditions, dispersion, speed of manoeuvre, suppressing fire and the use of cover were of paramount importance. Not all of these lessons were learnt immediately, however, and many men would fall in this and even the subsequent world war before they were truly taken to heart. Yet in incipient ways, the commanders of all combatants began to look for technological and tactical advantages that would carry their men more safely across no-man's-land.

Verdun and the Somme

On 6 December 1915, Allied (i.e. the Entente Powers) commanders – including representatives from Russia – met for a conference at Chantilly, north of Paris. The purpose of the meeting was to find a co-ordinated way of breaking the deadlock into which the war had evidently descended. It was decided that the only way to transform the situation was through common, simultaneous action on multiple fronts, as the French memorandum following the conference made clear:

> The Allied armies ought to resume the general offensive on the Franco-British, Italian and Russian fronts as soon as they are in a state to do so. All the efforts of the Coalition must be exerted in the preparation and execution of this decisive action, which will only produce its full effect as a co-ordination of offensives.

By attacking on multiple fronts, it was hoped that the German defensive capabilities would simply be overwhelmed, precipitating a general collapse of the Kaiser's army. For the Western Front, the

4. The infamous 'first day of the Somme' was announced by the explosion of a mine at Hawthorn Ridge on 1 July 1916 at 0730hrs. This day remains one of the bloodiest in the history of the British Army. Photograph taken by Ernest Brooks. Crown Copyright/Public Domain.

Douglas Haig (1861–1928)

Douglas Haig, more than any other individual, is publicly identified with the controversy and bloodshed of the First World War. Educated at Oxford, he joined the Royal Military Academy at Sandhurst in 1884 before receiving a commission as a British Army cavalry officer. He served in various colonial territories and experienced combat in the Sudan campaign (1897–98) and the Boer War (1899–1902), before becoming the director of military training at the War Office in 1906. With the onset of war in 1914, he took command of I Army Corps in the BEF, then became commander-in-chief in December 1916, in charge of sixty-two divisions. Haig was a dogged and forceful character, who frequently struggled in building relationships with politicians and allies. History has frequently cast Haig in an unfavourable light, particularly in terms of an apparently dismissive relationship to massive British casualties. Yet in balance, his strategic choices were often limited by obligations to the French. He served as commander-in-chief of the British Army until 1921, when he retired from military service.

5. *Sir Douglas Haig.*

intention was to launch a combined Anglo-French offensive in Picardy, along the River Somme (the Somme formed the junction between the British and the French armies). The offensive was scheduled for mid-August 1916 and would be delivered on a grand scale, using twenty-five British divisions and thirty-nine French. Haig would also be the man in charge of the British effort – he had replaced John French as the British commander-in-chief of the BEF on 10 December after the failed attack at Loos.

Plans for the Somme offensive were thrown into the air by an unexpected turn of events. On 21 February 1916, the Germans launched a vast offensive against the French at Verdun, south of the Somme front. The epic ten-month battle cost more than 600,000 lives and, although it eventually turned into a close-run French victory, it stripped the French of huge reserves of manpower. To relieve the pressure while fighting was under way, Haig was pushed into bringing forward the Somme offensive by six weeks, with the British now in the lead role.

The Battle of the Somme, which began on 1 July 1916, has gone down in history as one of Britain's bloodiest campaigns. After a week-long bombardment of German lines by 1,500

6. '"Hecatombs" sacrificed to the moloch of Prussian militarism: massed German infantry attacking at Verdun mown down by the French guns.' This version of the attack at Verdun was drawn by Frédéric de Haenen. The Illustrated War News, 29 March 1916.

guns firing 1.7 million shells, two British and two French armies attacked across a 20-mile front. Although the French made better progress in the south, the British were confronted by an appalling wall of machine-gun and artillery fire, and barbed-wire defensive systems remained intact, despite the shelling. The result was a massacre in no-man's-land. We have already noted the first-day and campaign casualty totals above, which were sustained for negligible gains. The British public was truly shocked by the casualty figures, which decimated the male population of entire communities by virtue of the regional identity of many of the British Army's battalions and regiments.

Yet the Battle of the Somme was also a punishing experience for the Germans who faced it. German casualties have been estimated as high as 600,000, and the German military leadership decided that their lines on the Western Front needed rationalising if the army was to sustain an effective defence. Here our story begins to connect in

7. The British line as of April 1916. The Illustrated War News, 5 April 1916.

BUNKERS

The Germans were masters at digging ferro-concrete underground bunkers. They were at least 30–40ft below ground, accessible by concrete steps, and the best examples were fitted with telephones to the outside world, sewerage and drainage systems, central heating and even piped water. The occupants were virtually immune from any outside bombardment.

earnest with the future Battle of Cambrai. From September 1916, the Germans began construction of a new, shorter (by 30 miles) and stronger defensive line further back from the Somme positions. Known to the Allies as the 'Hindenburg Line' and by the Germans as the *Siegfried Stellung*, it ran from Arras to near Verdun and featured complex and defiant networks of trenches, dugouts, concrete bunkers, barbed wire and other defensive features. The Hindenburg Line, which the Germans occupied in March 1917, was a symptom of the fact that the German Army had indeed been hurt by the Somme offensive. However, it was also, by virtue of its impressive strength and more defensible qualities, a challenge to Allied victory on the Western Front.

The Road to Cambrai

The Battle of Cambrai came at the end of a long period of bloodletting in 1917. The Canadians took the strategically important position of Vimy Ridge between 9 and 12 April, albeit at high cost. A further boost to Allied morale came with the Battle of Messines the following June, when the Allies took the Messines Ridge strongpoint south of Ypres following an epic artillery bombardment and the detonation of a series of huge underground mines beneath the German lines.

Building on this success, and confident that the Germans were near to collapse, Haig then pursued a major summer campaign,

8. 'By Hindenburg's orders: "To be held at all costs": Passchendaele Ridge stormed by the Canadians.' Drawn by R. Caton Woodville. The Illustrated London News, 1 December 1917.

the Third Battle of Ypres. Its overarching objective was to reach the Belgian coast and take the German U-boat bases there (the UK was at that time suffering under Germany's policy of unrestricted submarine warfare). This battle was in horrifying contrast to the two others that preceded it. What became known as the Battle of Passchendaele, after the village that formed a key Allied objective, was an experience unimaginable to those who had not been there. It was launched on 31 July after 4 million Allied artillery shells had ploughed into the enemy defences. Exceptional summer rains, however, meant that the battlefield became a sucking morass that eventually drowned both men and even horses, and made every yard of advance a human nightmare. German reinforcements released from the Eastern Front bolstered the defenders, and the casualties amongst the British and Commonwealth troops reached simply appalling levels. Haig pushed on the offensive in bloody-minded fashion, against swelling public concern, until 6 November, claiming success with the capture of Passchendaele village. The small rewards nevertheless seemed well beneath the human cost of 310,000 men, and Haig's reputation began to wobble at home and at the front.

Even as the tragedy of Third Ypres was under way, the planning for a new, radically different offensive was evolving. The Cambrai sector of the Western Front lay roughly 50 miles to the south of Ypres, and during the spring of 1917 Haig and others were already eyeing the area as a potential breakthrough point on the Hindenburg Line. Haig verbally commissioned III Corps, Fourth Army, to study such an operation, but the actual origin of the Cambrai offensive came from a variety of sources gathered into a single plan. Indeed, in the *Official History* of the campaign, Lieutenant General Sir Launcelot Kiggell, Haig's Chief of General Staff, stated that he couldn't really remember a specific start date for the planning of Cambrai.

Several key figures underpinned the development of the Cambrai plan. Central to its emergence was General the Hon. Sir Julian Byng, commander of the Third Army. The Third Army had been deployed to the quieter front south of Arras while the Ypres battle played itself out further north, and Byng was eager to find some way to make a meaningful contribution to the war. He inherited earlier plans for a Cambrai offensive from III Corps, but looked for ways to develop it into a more convincing proposal.

At this point, two other figures enter the picture. The first was Lieutenant Colonel J.F.C. Fuller, one of the landmark figures in the history of armoured warfare. At this time, he was GSO1 (General Staff Officer (Grade 1)) in the Tank Corps (the development and organisation of the Tank Corps is explored in depth in the next chapter); Brigadier General Hugh Elles was the head of the corps. Fuller, aware that tanks were proving to be little short of a liability on the muddy terrain of Ypres, argued that British armour could be used more effectively if suitable ground was chosen.

After some fits and starts, and blunt guidance from Elles, Fuller sketched out a proposal for a forty-eight-hour tank raid on the Cambrai front, where the untouched chalky ground and gently rolling terrain was ideally suited to tank movement. Some 200 tanks were to be involved in the attack between Banteux and Ribécourt, driving to the St Quentin canal. The objectives were strictly limited: destroy large numbers of German guns, take German soldiers prisoner (or inflict casualties) and then return back to friendly lines. Fuller submitted his ideas to the General Headquarters (GHQ) as a formal plan. On its own, however, Fuller's plan for a tank raid was not sufficiently persuasive. It would take the arrival of another proposal at GHQ to fulfil Fuller's dream of a massed armoured engagement.

Brigadier General Hugh H. Tudor was, like Fuller, a forward-looking man. He was also the artillery commander of 9th (Scottish) Division, IV Corps, and invested much of his intellectual effort in transforming artillery from a blunt instrument to a battle-winning tool. Tudor also conceived of a large-scale raid in the Cambrai sector, again using tanks, but he situated the armour within a far more coherent attack structure. Tudor recognised that the very act of delivering a preparatory bombardment, preceded itself by registering the guns on enemy lines, served as an emphatic warning to the Germans that an infantry attack would follow shortly. As had been proved in past offensives, the Germans were durable masters at sitting out a bombardment in their deep dugouts, then emerging when the guns fell silent to meet the British infantry with rifle and machine-gun fire. Yet Tudor was at the forefront of new artillery techniques in which the guns could be set on the target without firing a shot, known as 'map shooting' (see the following chapter), thereby offering the possibility of a sudden, devastating surprise bombardment delivered simultaneously with a ground assault.

Preparatory bombardments also often failed in their objective of cutting enemy barbed-wire defences, although, as historian Bryn Hammond has pointed out, the introduction of the No.106

9. An illustration from a German newspaper of German soldiers repairing a telephone wire in their communication trench – note the depth of the trench walls. The Illustrated War News, 29 March 1916.

instantaneous fuse in 1917 made the explosive severing of barbed wire far more efficient. Tanks, however, were a more straightforward and direct method of dealing with barbed-wire obstructions – they could simply roll over and crush the wire beneath their caterpillar tracks or drag it out of the way.

Tudor took the map-shooting techniques and armour opportunities and combined them into a raid of futuristic brilliance. Surprise was critical. The German lines at Cambrai would come under a sudden, terrifying deluge of smoke and high explosives, behind which heavy armour would advance to roll over the barbed-wire defences, opening the way for exploitation by infantry and cavalry, and a push through the Hindenburg Line. Tudor's plan was handled with interest by the IV Corps commander, Lieutenant General Sir Charles Woollcombe, who passed it on to the Third Army GHQ.

Although the chronological steps by which the Cambrai plan took shape are uncertain, what is clear is that the ideas of Fuller and Tudor coalesced within the Third Army high command. Elles was brought to the Cambrai front to reconnoitre the ground in terms of its suitability for tank warfare, and gave a positive assessment. Byng, himself a former cavalryman, was inspired by the idea that once the artillery and tanks had made the breakthrough, the British Cavalry Corps could flood through the gaps, harrying the German retreat and cutting deep into their lines of communication.

Eventually the battle plan reached Haig in September 1917. He was also impressed with the boldness and the enterprise of the scheme. Haig prevaricated for a month, waiting to see how the Ypres offensive unfolded, but by mid-October it was clear that there would be no great victory there. So Haig placed new hope in the Cambrai plan and authorised its launch for November. Now the ideas of people such as Fuller, Elles, Byng and Tudor would be realised on the ground.

THE ARMIES

The Battle of Cambrai was really a clash of two armies: General Sir Julian Byng's Third Army and, across the wire, General Georg von der Marwitz's Second Army, which in turn fell under the responsibility of Kronprinz Rupprecht of Bavaria, the commander of the German Army Group North. It should be noted that for both the British and the Germans, the Cambrai sector was often used as a region in which battle-wearied units and formations could be rested with comparatively minor combat commitments. Von der Marwitz's Second Army was nineteen divisions strong, the bulk of these divisions being regular infantry formations. The heart of the German Army was the regiment, which much like British battalions and regiments were often raised on a regional basis (although war casualties over time eroded the regional identity of any formation). When the war began in 1914, the typical German Army infantry division consisted of four regiments, but in the spring of 1915 rising casualties and the demands of fighting on multiple fronts led to the creation of three-regiment divisions. Further reorganisation in 1916–17 reduced the number of riflemen in a platoon to around fifty, compared to eighty-one in 1914. To compensate for the reduction in manpower, the firepower allocated to a rifle company was increased, including light machine-gun teams for each platoon and hand- and rifle-grenade sections at company level.

General Georg von der Marwitz (1856–1929)

Georg von der Marwitz is a legendary figure in the history of First World War commanders. Born in 1856 in Pomerania, he joined the German Army in 1875 in General Staff positions, but then rose through regimental, corps and divisional commands. Von der Marwitz was at heart a cavalryman, and by 1913 he was the Inspector General of Cavalry. His initial role in the First World War was to lead a cavalry group in Belgium, and although he suffered an early defeat in this role – at Haelen on 12 August 1914 – his subsequent leadership earned him promotion, respect and decorations. His wartime career was characterised by great diversity, both in terms of the formations he led and the theatres in which he fought. He headed formations such as the II Cavalry Corps, XXXVIII Reserve Corps, VI Army Corps, the Beskiden Corps (Ski Corps) and the Second Army (which he handled at the Battle of Cambrai), fighting on both the Western and Eastern Fronts. His performance against the Russians at battles such as Second Masuria (7–21 February 1915) and Gorlice-Tarnow (2–10 May 1915) brought him the Pour le Mérite and Oak Leaves, but combat on the Western Front offered greater challenges, as it was unsuited to the use of cavalry and manoeuvre. His reputation as a tough and innovative commander was cemented at Cambrai in November 1917, yet in 1918 he suffered the initial high point and then the cruel collapse of German forces during their summer offensives against the Allies. Following the German defeat, von der Marwitz retired in December 1918. He died in 1929, having had an exceptional military career undone only by the general collapse of Germany's strength.

10. Von der Marwitz shown here on the right with the Kaiser on his way to inspect troops.

Trench mortar, flamethrower and pioneer sections at regimental level also stiffened the assault capability of the German units, despite the steady reduction in personnel since the beginning of the war. Indeed, one of the strengths of the German Army – proven in its late-war offensives of 1918 – was the development of fast assault tactics, something that it would use to its advantage in the Battle of Cambrai.

Although a total of three German corps were in the Cambrai sector at the time of the British offensive, only one – XIII, known as *Gruppe Caudry* – was actually occupying the positions on which the attack would fall. It consisted of four divisions (from north to south): 20th *Landwehr* Division, 54th Infantry Division, 9th Reserve Division and 183rd Infantry Division. The combat capability of these formations was mixed, with the 20th *Landwehr* Division being the weakest of the bunch, and their artillery support was limited. Yet they were 'secure in the knowledge that despite their weakness on the ground the great Hindenburg defences effectively sheltered them' (Woollcombe, p.61).

The British offensive at Cambrai would be launched by III and IV Corps of Byng's Third Army. IV Corps was commanded by Lieutenant General Sir Charles Woollcombe, while III Corps was led by Lieutenant General Sir William Pulteney. Each division was subdivided according to the structure typical by 1917: three brigades, each four battalions strong. A battalion theoretically had a strength of 30 officers and 1,000 men, although the realities of war often whittled the actual complement down to significantly fewer. At this period in British Army history, regiments and battalions also had an extremely regional identity. For example, the 35th Brigade of the 12th (Eastern) Division, part of III Corps, consisted of the following battalions: 7th Norfolks, 7th Suffolks, 9th Essex and 5th Royal Berks, each with its own clear regional links. Yet, as with the German units and formations, the war had often diluted the regional homogeneity of battalions, and by 1917 a battalion's men could come from a mixture of locales back in the UK. Note also that whereas the German infantryman had a

General Sir Julian Byng (1862–1935)

By the time he reached the Battle of Cambrai in November 1917, General Sir Julian Hedworth George Byng had already accrued an impressive reputation as a military commander. His army career began in the militia in the 1870s, and he rose to the rank of lieutenant in the King's Royal Rifle Corps in 1882. Byng acquired expeditionary combat experience in Egypt, the Sudan and during the Boer War, and he then entered the regular army and began a steady climb through rank and influence. Known as 'Bungo' to his close friends, Byng was a charismatic and intelligent commander, and by the outbreak of war in 1914 he was ranked major general and was commander of British forces in Egypt. With war declared, he returned home to command the 3rd Cavalry Division and then the entire Cavalry Corps of the BEF. For his leadership at the Third Battle of Ypres, Byng was awarded the Order of St Michael and St George as a Knight Commander. In May 1915, he was sent to command IX Corps in the disastrous Gallipoli campaign; although this campaign wrecked several officers' careers, Byng came out of it with further credit after supervising the successful withdrawal. He was appointed commander of the Canadian Corps in 1916, and the corps' victory at Vimy Ridge in April 1917 brought Byng a full generalship. He then took charge of Third Army, which he famously led at the Battle of Cambrai, and the rest of his wartime

service brought further victories. After the war, Byng served in several high official positions, including as Governor General of Canada (1921–26) and as commissioner of the London Metropolitan Police (1928–31).

11. Sir Julian Byng.

primary loyalty to his regiment, for the British soldier it was the battalion to which he owed his affiliation, a reflection of the British Army's smaller, more expeditionary outlook as opposed to the German Army's continental thinking.

The British and Commonwealth soldiers would enjoy the support of powerful artillery resources at the Battle of Cambrai. Indeed, historians such as Bryn Hammond have argued, with justification, that in many ways Cambrai was an artillery battle more than a tank battle. There were three main elements to British Army artillery. Frontline artillery support was provided by the Royal Horse Artillery (RHA) and Royal Field Artillery (RFA), operating light- and medium-calibre pieces that commanded typical ranges of 5,000–7,000yds. The heavy-calibre, long-range guns were the responsibility of the Royal Garrison Artillery (RGA). These guns were set behind the frontline, and with calibres of around 13in they could send heavy fire out to ranges of more than 13,000yds. All elements of the British Army artillery would be present at the Battle of Cambrai, and in total more than 1,000 guns would be acting in support.

To the infantry assault was added the full weight of the British Army's Tank Corps, led by Hugh Elles. (The Tank Corps had been titled the Heavy Branch, Machine Gun Corps, but was retitled just before the Battle of Messines in June 1917.) A total of 476 tanks would roll into action at Cambrai, by far the greatest assemblage

HORSES

Although motor vehicles were used in reasonable numbers as artillery tractors, the bulk of artillery haulage was performed by horses. Indeed, horses were the primary means of logistics for all armies in the First World War, as they had better traction over rough or muddy ground than contemporary wheeled vehicles. Deployed in vast numbers to the frontline, they suffered accordingly – an estimated 8 million horses died during the war.

12. The original caption for this image commented that 'the war horse is not yet extinct'. However, the birth of tank warfare did mean its days were numbered. The War Budget, 13 April 1916.

of armour the world had ever seen. The Tank Corps was divided into three brigades, with the 1st Tank Brigade (108 vehicles) allocated to support the 51st and 62nd Divisions of IV Corps, while the 2nd and 3rd Tank Brigades (216 tanks) were given to the 6th, 12th and 20th Divisions of III Corps.

While the artillery gave firepower, the tanks breached the wire and the infantry took the enemy defences, it was left to the Cavalry Corps to exploit the gaps made in the enemy defence. The cavalry had so far had a somewhat frustrating war. As subsequent analysis will show, horse-mounted warriors still offered one of the best means of fast battlefield manoeuvre, despite their somewhat archaic appearance on an industrialised battlefield. Yet opportunities for making a battle-changing contribution had been limited. As the war progressed, the cavalry rarely fought en masse from horseback, but their undoubted mobility meant that they could still deploy quickly and then dismount to fight as shock infantry.

The solid terrain of Cambrai offered the cavalry a fresh opportunity for glory. The Cavalry Corps was commanded by

13. Soldiers of the Machine Gun Corps. The Library of Congress.

Lieutenant General Sir Charles Kavanagh and it consisted of no less than five cavalry divisions. It was given responsibility for pushing through the Hindenburg Line once broken, moving quickly through to isolate Cambrai itself, take the Bourlon Ridge, and go on to sever the German lines of communication between Cambrai and Arras. What would be critical was that the German barbed-wire defences were taken out prior to the cavalry being committed to battle, otherwise the men and horses would likely be held up and slaughtered.

The orders of battle of the German and British forces around Cambrai gave some measure of confidence to Byng's staff. The Third Army, Tank Corps, Cavalry Corps and other formations brought more than twenty divisions to the field, plus tactics that, if surprise could be maintained before the launch of the offensive, would give the British control of the battle's tempo from the outset.

The Soldiers

The armies of 1917 on the Western Front were not those of 1914. At the beginning of the war, millions had joined the armed forces with enthusiasm, the flame of patriotism fanned by localised enlistment that saw entire communities shipped off to the front to fight alongside one another. Patriotism and commitment were far from dead by 1917, but the armies themselves had suffered scything losses. The British (not counting Commonwealth and colonial servicemen) had, by the time of Cambrai, lost more than 700,000 dead. For the Germans, who had been fighting on two fronts, the depletions were far worse. In total, the German Empire would lose more than 2 million men during the war, and the death toll was certainly well beyond 1 million in November 1917.

The crucial point is that while both sides had poured out rivers of blood, the British were better placed to make good their losses and keep the war effort going, for on 6 April 1917 the United States declared war on Germany, meaning that the British now had the huge American manpower reserves coming into play at a late stage of the war. Germany had no such good fortune and instead had to use its remaining soldiery in the most meaningful way.

The German Army was, like the British, composed of several different types of soldier: active (regular), reservist, *Landwehr* and *Landsturm*, the last two in the list being territorial and second-line reservists of uncertain quality. Socially, the officer class was dominated by the *Junkers*, the landed nobility of Prussia and East Germany, while the rank and file were, appropriately, weighted in favour of rural manpower. Even though the cities did provide huge numbers of soldiers for the German war effort, the urban populations tended to be a little more political and left-leaning, which made their loyalty to the Kaiser rather more suspect.

At the base level, a German infantry unit was centred upon an eight- or nine-man *Gruppe*, of which there were two in a *Korporalschaften* (section). There were four of these sections

The German Soldier at Cambrai

The individual German soldier was, generally speaking, an effective instrument of war. The German Army invested heavily in training, resulting in men who could display independence of action once the conditions of battle isolated them from higher orders. This focus also helped the army produce elite units of assault troops, such as the famous *Stoßtruppen* and the pioneers, who were experts in the tactical handling of assault weapons such as mortars, flamethrowers and poison gas. The German soldier was also extremely capable in defence, skilled in the use of the Mauser Gewehr 98 rifle and the MG08 machine-gun. Yet not all German soldiers were elite; far from it. Many of the late-war formations were of an indifferent quality, particularly those of a reserve or territorial nature. At Cambrai, for example, the 20th *Landwehr* Division was of shaky substance. It had been formed in September 1916, and was composed of one-third men who were recovered wounded and two-thirds *Landsturm* soldiers who had previously worked in supply services in Belgium. It was not the most convincing of compositions. The 9th Reserve Division, by contrast, had seen periodic combat since the beginning of the war and was a far more dependable formation. It had nevertheless taken heavy casualties during the fighting of summer 1917 and consequently was sent to the Cambrai sector for rest and reorganisation (it found the latter, but certainly not the former). The German soldiers at Cambrai were therefore a product of both training and war, with mixed abilities and experience, but backed by a strong system of command and some extremely well-trained units.

14. German infantry line up on the edge of a forest. War of the Nations, New York Times Co., New York, 1919.

in a *Zug* (platoon), and three platoons within a *Kompanie* (company). Firepower support was provided by regimental and independent machine-gun companies, plus regimental artillery. Note also that various regiments and divisions could be formed into improvised *Gruppen* (groups), typically governed by a corps headquarters. The *Gruppe* system was an organisational success of both world wars, allowing the high command to form new formations to meet the requirements of the battle.

In terms of the command structure of the German Army, it was more centralised than its British opponents, with a complicated chain of command and constant supervision of the men by the officers and NCOs. (German Army units had three times as many NCOs as equivalent British units.) This command network could cause problems in itself, particularly when it came to issues such as the efficient control of artillery.

The British had some structural similarities to the German forces. Like the German Army, the British Army was a composite force, composed of regular, volunteer and reservist forces. Enlistment into the armed services was initially greater than anything the army structure could cope with, but it did decline annually during the war. In 1916, for example, 1.2 million men entered the army, but in 1917 the figure had dropped to 800,000. Factor in the casualty rates and the British Army's manpower was becoming squeezed by the time of the Battle of Cambrai.

The smallest core unit of the British Army was the twelve-man section, led by a corporal or sergeant. Each man in the section had a specialism, related to the weaponry he would deploy in action. By 1917 a typical frontline combat soldier was either a 'bomber' (deploying hard grenades), 'rifleman', 'Lewis gunner' or 'rifle grenadier' (skilled in using rifle-launched grenades). Four sections made up a platoon, four platoons a company, and four companies a battalion.

It is a myth of the war that the British soldier spent months on end in sodden frontline trenches. This did occur in isolated cases to certain unfortunate units, especially early in the war, but generally soldiers

The 'Tommy'

The British soldier or 'Tommy' took his place in a complicated society when he joined the army. At the beginning of the war, the upper classes easily dominated the officer ranks, but casualties and volunteerism diluted this imbalance. The professional middle classes came to occupy many officer and enlisted positions, particularly amongst the newly formed regional battalions. For example, in 1914 the founder of Burnley Lads' Club – mill owner H.D. Riley – used the club as the core of a Lads' Club Company, of which he became the commanding officer with no previous military experience. Historian William Turner quotes one of the eyewitnesses to the recruitment drive: 'Miners, mill-hands, office-boys, black-coats, bosses, school-boys and masters, found themselves appearing before Mr Ross and the medical officer … Men of mature age, patriotic or sensing adventure or to escape from monotony were ready to have a go at anyone who should pull the lion's tail' (William Turner, *Accrington Pals*, London, 1992, p.29).

For a regular soldier, training in the British Army could be a rather haphazard affair. Basic training would last in the region of two months and was typically focused upon field craft, bayonet drill and marksmanship. The gulf between theory and the reality of war could be profound, however. An important transitional stage, therefore, was when a unit made its first trip to the frontline, when the incumbent and therefore more experienced battalion would provide a few days of invaluable instruction in the realities of trench life and combat. Then it was up to each Tommy to learn how to survive, and fast.

15. One of the more popular recruiting posters of the era. The War Budget, 5 August 1915.

were rotated between frontline, support and reserve trenches, plus regular trips to the rear. As a general rule, only about four to eight days were spent in the frontline trenches before similar periods in the support and reserve trenches. Time spent in support and reserve positions (which ran roughly parallel to the frontline trench) was not without danger, however, as they were generally still within reach of long-range enemy artillery and the soldiers also had to make trips further forward to perform maintenance and supply duties.

Of course, infantrymen were not the only figures on the battlefield at Cambrai in 1917. The five divisions of the Cavalry Corps were very different creatures to the infantry. While the infantry were primarily tasked with the foot-slogging business of crossing no-man's-land and taking the enemy trench in a frontal assault, the cavalry were meant to move through gaps and weak flanks, providing the rapid movement and decisive exploitations unavailable to the infantry. Herein lay a problem, as Richard Holmes has pointed out:

On the Western Front there were no open flanks round which cavalry could swirl, and the difficulties of moving troops, on foot or horseback, across crowded rear areas while a battle was in progress made it difficult to bring cavalry up in time to seize a fleeting opportunity

Holmes, *Tommy*, p.440

Holmes defines a problem that did indeed bedevil the cavalry arm during the war. It was certainly operating under conditions utterly different to those of the nineteenth century, when battlefields tended to be compact and infantry were concentrated rather than dispersed over huge areas. Much has therefore been written in popular literature about the failures of the cavalry in the First World War, about how the mounted soldier was an obsolescent disaster in a world of machine-guns, barbed wire and infantry. Thankfully, a small but diligent group of historians (Holmes included) have gone some way to abolishing this myth. There were certainly disastrous battles for the cavalry, but that was true for the infantry also.

16. As the war developed, entrenched cavalry found it harder to manouevre on the Western Front and the ever-present danger of barbed wire was an increasing threat that horsed cavalrymen found it difficult to overcome. Illustrated War News, Vol. 7, Illustrated London News & Sketch, London, 1918. Courtesy of www.gwpda.org.uk

Furthermore, while the cavalry did come from a traditional elite social background – a fact which has been highlighted by many casual historians – they still acknowledged the realities of the new world of warfare. Haig himself emphasised that cavalry needed to work in a combined-arms relationship with artillery, infantry and

---

LIFE EXPECTANCY

Junior officers serving on the Western Front in 1916–17 had a life expectancy in the region of six weeks. Such losses made continuity of command and training difficult for many frontline units, and as ever the NCO class became the glue that held many units together.

---

various other support weapons. For example, rather than being implacably opposed to the machine-gun, the cavalry formed dedicated brigade machine-gun squadrons in 1916, each consisting of six sections with two Vickers machine-guns in each. In turn, the machine-gun squadrons created a separate Machine Gun Corps (Cavalry) or MGC(C). Armoured cars and artillery were also fully integrated into the cavalry.

At the level of the individual cavalryman, tradition also sat side by side with modernity. While the French and German cavalry uniforms harked back to some of the impractical displays of the previous centuries, the British cavalry wore plain khaki uniforms and caps. Although they carried lance and sabre, they also utilised the standard infantry Short Magazine Lee-Enfield (SMLE) rifle. Nor were they wedded to their mounts in combat; training focused as much on dismounted combat as fighting from horseback. There is, however, no denying that the Cavalry Corps felt, by late 1917, that it still had to demonstrate the value of its mobility and dash. Many doubtless felt that the Battle of Cambrai would provide the opportunity.

Weapons

The First World War was a conflict in which the tools of war reached industrial levels of efficiency, in terms of their ability to repeat inexorably the killing process. Weaponry had truly begun its journey into modernity during the nineteenth century, with the introduction of breech-loading cartridge firearms, automatic weapons (in the form of Maxim's machine-gun), breech-loading artillery and more potent explosives. Although the new breeds of weapons were tested in warfare before 1914 in conflicts such as the Russo-Japanese War (1904–05), the First World War revealed the true extent of their power in a way the world had never witnessed.

In terms of rifles, the Germans and the British were similarly equipped with bolt-action weapons. The British carried the redoubtable 0.303in SMLE, first introduced into service in 1906. Measuring 44.57in long, the SMLE had many virtues, and was a true infantryman's rifle. It was robust in the field, with its wooden furniture extending all the way to the muzzle, giving the rifle a distinctive 'snub-nosed' appearance. It was fed via a ten-round box magazine, and its bolt-action mechanism was known for its speed and fluidity. In well-trained hands, the rifle could send out fifteen rounds per minute (rpm), with each of the powerful 0.303in bullets having a killing range of well over a mile. (Although there were snipers who engaged targets at long distances, most infantry would be conversant at shooting within ranges of 200–600yds.)

The German equivalent of the SMLE was the 7.92mm x 57mm Mauser Gewehr 98. The Mauser bolt-action mechanism was renowned for its safety and easy handling, but the rifle's internal box magazine could only hold half the number of rounds of the Lee-Enfield. An additional problem was that the standard iron sights fitted to the gun were graduated to a minimum of 400m (437yds), which was actually in excess of the typical ranges at which infantrymen fought. Nevertheless, Allied soldiers quickly learnt never to expose any part of their body above the trench line, as a Mauser-equipped sniper would quickly respond with an often fatal shot.

In terms of heavy firepower, the British utilised the 0.303in Vickers machine-gun, which was a water-cooled, recoil-operated version of the Maxim gun. The Vickers was a gun of astonishing reliability, with a rate of fire of 500rpm and a lethal range (using indirect fire) of more than 4,000yds. It was a physically demanding weapon to haul about and deploy (the gun alone

17. The Lewis machine gun was known as the 'hose of death'. The Illustrated War News, 3 May 1916.

weighed 40lb), however, and each gun was manned by six to eight men in total. German forces relied on the Maxim MG08 as their primary heavy machine-gun. Firing a 7.92mm round, its mode of operation and combat capabilities were roughly the same as the Vickers, and it too was enormously weighty – 69lb for the gun and its bulky sledge mount.

One problem with both the Vickers and the MG08 was that their bulk and weight made them unsuitable for use in the mobile assault phase of action. For this reason, both sides developed and used varieties of light machine-gun, weapons that were light enough to be carried and operated by one man. These firearms allowed infantry groups and sections to take their own fire support with them into the attack.

For the British, their light machine-gun of choice was the Lewis gun, a US-designed weapon recalibrated for British 0.303in ammunition. The Lewis weighed 25lb, could fire at 600rpm and was operated from an integral collapsible bipod. It was an air-cooled and gas-operated gun and, apart from the barrel jacket (which served to aid barrel cooling), its most distinctive feature was its flat forty-seven- or ninety-seven-round drum magazine. Being generally reliable and easy to use, Lewis guns had transformed British Army infantry firepower at the section level by 1917, with each section having a Lewis gunner, thereby making a total of forty-six Lewis guns per battalion.

German forces also had their own breeds of light machine-gun, although the type was never quite as successfully adopted as the Lewis. The nearest equivalent to the Lewis was the Bergmann MG15 nA, an air-cooled weapon introduced into service in 1916, albeit in limited numbers and primarily on the Italian front. It was mounted on a bipod and fired from a 200-round aluminium link belt, a belt design that was quite advanced for the time. Because of its relatively small numbers, and problems with overheating after firing about 300 rounds, the MG15 nA was not very influential on the Western Front. Germany's major attempt at a light machine-gun, therefore, was the MG08/15. This weapon was essentially a modified MG08, fitted with a bipod, pistol grip and shoulder stock, but retaining a water-coolant jacket around the barrel. The MG08/15 carried the reliability and performance of its parent weapon, yet its weight was a little too much for the light machine-gun type – 36lb with its water jacket full. Such weight limited its battlefield mobility, but there is no doubt that German units applied them to good effect to deliver portable suppressing fire at key points on the battlefield.

Machine-guns and rifles formed the basic arsenal of the British and German infantry, but the requirements of trench fighting in particular demanded other types of weapon. Bayonets were a standard, and psychologically intimidating, addition to the rifle, fitted around or beneath the muzzle. The bayonet was a close-quarters weapon and was given a particularly manly status, being indicative of the desire to close with and fight with the enemy face to face in the 'offensive spirit'. Contemporary bayonets were certainly disquieting pieces of steel. The 1907 Pattern Wilkinson Sword bayonet was no less than 17in long, and could skewer the average man through from front to back. The main German bayonet – the M1898 Short – had a blade of just 11.4in, but this was actually a

18. German machine-gunners in action. The Illustrated War News, 12 April 1916.

more efficient combat tool; early war experience showed that the longer types often became stuck inside an unfortunate victim and couldn't be retracted easily.

Those facing a bayonet charge needed strong nerves and an aggression equal to that of the attackers, but in reality bayonets actually inflicted relatively few casualties. Part of the problem was that wielding just the rifle alone in the narrow confines of a trench could be problematic enough without extending the rifle's length by fitting a bayonet. For this reason, soldiers on both sides resorted to a variety of improvised trench weapons that rivalled medieval arsenals in terms of their grim design. Nail-spiked clubs, knuckle-dusters, sharpened spades, hatchets – all manner of hacking creations were put into play. Such weapons must have turned close-quarters trench combat into a singular horror.

19. *Bayonet practice. This exercise in Toronto was part of a recruiting drive, however at close-quarters the bayonet could be a very deadly weapon. The Illustrated War News, 5 April 1916.*

There were other, more modern, weapons ideally suited to trench combat. Hand grenades, for example, were the perfect option for clearing a section of trench, a dugout or a bunker. In fact, the grenade was the primary trench-clearance device and at the heart of infantry tactics. In 1915 the classic No.5 Mills bomb (known after its inventor, William Mills) entered service. This 1.25lb fragmentation grenade fitted comfortably in the hand, had a four- or seven-second fuse delay and a lethal radius of 5–10yds. It worked and worked well, and in 1917 an improved version (the No.36M) was produced, which had greater durability in the field and could be fired from a rifle-grenade discharger.

The Germans had a far wider variety of grenades in service than the British and their allies. Types included the *Stielhandgranate* (stick grenade), the *Diskushandgranate* (disc grenade), *Eierhandgranate* (hand grenade) and *Kugelhandgranate* (ball grenade). The Model 24 *Stielhandgranate* is the most popularly known type on account of its distinctive design – the explosive

HOME-MADE GRENADES

The British began the war with extremely limited stocks of inefficient Mk I grenades, and soldiers resorted to home-made devices using tin cans and glass pots stuffed with gun cotton or dynamite and crude pieces of shrapnel, fitted with a basic fuse.

charge was fixed in a metal canister on the end of a long wooden handle, the friction-ignited fuse of the grenade running through the handle. A key advantage of the handle was that the thrower could apply greater leverage to achieve greater distance. A thrower with a good arm could hurl the *Stielhandgranate* up to 30yds, twice the distance of a Mills bomb.

Of course, the distance to which grenades could be delivered could be dramatically improved by using a rifle, rather than a human arm, as a discharger. Rifle grenades, depending on the variety, were typically launched by either slotting a rod, integral to the grenade, down the barrel of the gun or placing a grenade in a cup discharger similarly fitted to the barrel. Firing a blank cartridge from the gun then launched the grenade to distances of up to 200yds. In terms of practice regarding rifle grenades, the two sides diverged. The British used them throughout the war, but the German largely abandoned them in 1916. Rifle grenades were inaccurate, slow to use and could damage the rifle through imparting excessive recoil, so their overall value is certainly open to question. In skilled hands, however, they could give an infantryman his own minor form of indirect-fire artillery, which had an obvious utility in trench warfare.

Kit and Uniform

The conditions of the First World War tested the legendary hardiness of the wartime generation to the limit. Not only did soldiers have to endure direct, constant exposure to the year-round elements, but they also had to act as beasts of burden, carrying the extensive and heavy standard kit, as well as many other tools, weapons and devices.

The realities of wartime economies, and the need to equip huge standing armies, forced the combatants of the First World War to adopt uniforms and kit that were strictly utilitarian in nature and function. For the German Army, this meant shedding some of the last vestiges of imperial appearance. The topic of German Army uniform is too large to deal with in detail here, but a simple comparison between the common infantryman of 1914 and that of 1917 is informative. The soldier of 1914 was clad in the 1910 *Feldgrau* (field grey) tunic and trousers, and shod his feet in calf-length leather jackboots. The M1907 greatcoat provided outer warmth in cold conditions. In addition to the visor-less *Feldmütze* (field cap), worn during general duties, the M1895 *Pickelhaube* helmet was the most nationally defining item – it consisted of a boiled leather shell with brass fittings and a prominent decorative spike sticking up from the crown. In terms of load-carrying equipment, the soldier of 1914 would typically rely on the cow-hide M1895 knapsack and the cloth M1887 haversack (often known as the 'breadbag'). For ammunition, the soldier had a belt of six leather M1909 cartridge pouches, each pouch holding four five-round clips of 7.92mm ammunition. Other items carried to war included the M1892 tent cloth, M1907 water bottle and black aluminium M1910 mess tin.

Although the M1910 uniform and associated kit were improvements on previous generations of German military apparel, they still left much to be desired. By many accounts, and even when shrouded in a cloth cover during combat, the *Pickelhaube* was a ludicrously impractical battlefield helmet, and gave little protection to the wearer against bullet and shrapnel. The M1895 knapsack was uncomfortable under combat conditions, and held up poorly in wet weather. Furthermore, state and regimental variations in tunic design were to the detriment of wartime economies of production.

For such reasons, the German Army infantry uniform went through several phases of rationalisation and simplification during the war. (Note: although the following description is accurate, the cost savings of re-use meant that early war items of clothing and kit would be seen for the duration of the conflict, apart from the helmet.) Looking at the soldier of 1917, he was wearing the all-arms *Bluse* campaign tunic, with virtually all elements of colour purged from the uniform. The most distinctive change was that the *Pickelhaube* was gone, replaced in 1916 by the far more credible M1916 *Stahlhelm* (steel helmet), a substantial nickel-steel helmet that provided excellent protection to skull and neck. Load-carrying straps had been blackened, and a more convenient and comfortable *Sturmgepäck* (assault pack) carried essential gear, albeit still alongside the M1887 haversack. Many other items had seen minor wartime modifications, although this did not always equate with improvement; the materials with which uniforms were made generally declined in quality as the war went on, as economic hardship bit in Germany. Nevertheless, the German Army uniform came to be both practical and modern, separated from its imperial ancestors by the reality of modern warfare.

The British Army uniform, helmet and kit also underwent changes to adapt to wartime conditions. Yet on the whole, the British and similarly clad Commonwealth infantryman began the war with an acceptably modern standard of military clothing. The standard uniform was the 1902 Pattern Service Dress, which featured a khaki tunic with four button-down patch pockets (including an internal pocket under the tunic flap, usually containing a field dressing), plus matching khaki trousers. (A cheaper version of the tunic was produced from 1914, known as the 'Utility Tunic'.) The trousers tucked into long cloth puttees, wound from the top of the boot to just below the knee, and the standard footwear was the reversed-hide B5 ammunition boots, with metal-studded soles.

The British Army's headgear also went through a major evolution. In the first two years of the war, the soldier wore field caps in service, either an earlier stiff-brimmed type or a later (and

Somme 1916 – Saved by the M1916 helmet

'… suddenly, with a great clanging thud, I was hit on the forehead and knocked flying onto the floor of the trench … a shrapnel bullet had hit my helmet with great violence, without piercing it, but sufficiently hard to dent it. If I had, as had been usual up until a few days previously, been wearing a cap, then the Regiment would have had one more man killed.'

Quoted in Jack Sheldon, *The German Army on the Somme 1914–1916* (Barnsley UK, Pen & Sword Military, 2007) p.219

cheaper) soft type known affectionately as a 'Gor Blimey' cap. Battlefield experience quickly illustrated the protective deficiencies of these items, so in early 1916 the 'Helmet, Steel, Mk I' was introduced, designed by John Leopold Brodie. Weighing 1.3lb, it was a pressed-steel helmet with a wide brim, leather liner and chin strap. Although it did not provide the neck protection of the German *Stahlhelm*, it still ensured that thousands of British soldiers avoided serious head injury or death.

One of the more advanced elements of the British soldier's kit was the 1908 Pattern webbing system. This was formed from a wide web belt and two thick braces, on which hung two ammunition pouches (each holding seventy-five rounds of 0.303in ammunition), a bayonet frog (leather sheath), entrenching tool handle attachment, entrenching tool head in a web cover, water bottle carrier, a small haversack and a large pack worn on the back. Although the haversack and backpack could be uncomfortable when worn for long periods, the webbing system itself was a practical way to distribute load over a soldier's body while limiting the disruption to his centre of gravity.

The uniforms and kit of First World War soldiers appear basic by the standards of today's equivalents, with their advanced load-

20. The new steel helmets were lauded in Britain and on the front. They were inserted with a padded leather band to help check the force of a blow. Factories (mainly manned by female war workers) were encouraged to get them to the front as soon as possible. The Illustrated War News, 3 May 1916.

21. Soldiers from the Northumberland Fusiliers relax after the Battle of St Eloi. Despite their new steel helmets, they still revel in 'booty' from the enemy – it was common for both sides to collect souvenirs, such as helmets, uniforms, spent cartridges and even weapons. The Illustrated War News, 3 May 1916.

SMALL BOX RESPIRATOR

The standard British gas mask from 1916 was the Small Box Respirator (SBR). It consisted of a waterproof mask fitted with eyepieces and a tin cylinder filled with filtering chemicals, through which the wearer breathed. The SBR was a dramatic improvement over previous versions, which included hood-like chemically treated 'smoke helmets' and, in the early part of the war, sanitary pads soaked with anti-gas chemicals and tied over the face and mouth.

carrying systems, body armour and cutting-edge camouflage and ergonomics. Yet ultimately they expressed a difficult balancing act between economic constraint and battlefield durability, and between combat demands and mass production. The fact was that the uniforms of the First World War met the needs of a hardened generation of soldiery, and met them reasonably well.

Tactics

For the British, the tactical challenges of 1917 were in many ways little different to those of 1915. In essence, the defining problem of any offensive action was how to get attacking infantry across the lethal space of no-man's-land as efficiently and quickly as possible, so that they could assault, enter and take the enemy trenches. Only once trenches or other defences were secured could the British forces make gaps in the enemy line and exploit them.

Even though a stretch of no-man's-land might be less than 100yds long, the obstacles to crossing were formidable. The terrain itself was one barrier, as the rough passage of war and weather across its surface often left it cratered, muddy and strewn with detritus, all of which slowed down heavily laden infantry. (Third Ypres had been a particularly tortuous illustration of this effect.)

Then there were the infamous belts of barbed wire to negotiate. These defences did not consist of a thin straggle of wire, such as we see bordering farm land. Instead they were dense and complex hedgerows of twisted, rusty wire many yards deep (German barbed-wire systems in front of the Hindenburg Line in 1917 were up to 100yds deep). They were not only designed to slow and stop attacking infantry – and thereby provide defending machine-gunners with stationary targets – they were also laid out in great slanting angles to channel attackers on to the guns of their enemies. Little wonder, therefore, that the barbed wire of both sides was often strewn with the lonely remains of their enemies.

There was no way around it – wire had to be breached in order for the attackers to survive long enough to achieve their objectives. Prior to Cambrai, the British tackled barbed wire in several ways, all of varying efficiency. The most devastating effort was the preparatory artillery barrage, pounding the barbed wire with high explosives and shrapnel, hopefully blasting gaps in the wire or at least thinning the defences. The experience of battles such as the Somme in 1916 had taught that barbed-wire clearance by artillery – even artillery of great intensity and duration – rarely succeeded on its own. Instead, it could redistribute the wire into even worse labyrinthine patterns, as well as making the ground around it more unmanageable for swift advance. Furthermore, the bombardment simply alerted the defenders that an assault was in preparation, and that the zones being pounded were the likely sectors of the eventual attack. All of this meant cutting barbed wire was often done by the most basic of means – hand-held wire cutters. Performing this action on a 'live' battlefield, under the pre-ranged machine-guns and artillery of the enemy, must have been a terrifying experience.

Artillery

We shall return to barbed wire shortly, as its challenge intersects with the development of the tank, but more needs to be said of the use of artillery, and how the Germans responded to it. Cutting wire was only one objective of a preparatory bombardment. The other purposes were suppression and attrition. Suppressive fire worked by keeping the enemy hunkered down in their bunkers and trenches, while also hopefully killing troops in large numbers from a safe distance. Once the artillery barrage lifted, it was essential that the infantry attacked quickly, crossing no-man's-land before the Germans could recover, man their weapons and start sending out lethal streams of bullets into the advancing ranks. This was easier said than done. The Germans, given the manpower pressures of a two-front war, were largely more defensively minded before 1918 and constructed impressive ferro-concrete dugouts and bunkers, often sunk tens of metres below the battlefield's surface. Machine-gunners and other key occupants of the trenches could ride out a firestorm beneath ground (although the experience would certainly be harrowing), then emerge quickly to set up their weapons the moment the barrage stopped.

22. Here a French artillery bombardment has done it's job on a section of German trench, near Verdun. *The Illustrated War News, 22 March 1916.*

23. A solidly constructed concrete dugout in a captured section of German trench, near Ypres. The Illustrated War News, 22 March 1916.

Barrages could be varied in manner to try to outwit countermeasures. The word 'barrage' is simplistic in popular terminology, yet the applications of barrages greatly exercised British minds throughout the war. The most basic sort of barrage was the 'standing barrage', in which the artillery simply pounded a fixed target, such as a trench line. 'Box barrages' bracketed a position on two or three sides, and served to prevent reinforcements from flooding into a beleaguered position. A more complex artillery variation was the 'creeping barrage', whereby the impact zone was advanced in timed increments (such as pushed forward 50yds every minute), with the infantry advancing closely behind. Timing and precise artillery/infantry co-ordination were critical here. The objective was to deny the enemy adequate recovery time before the infantry descended upon their trenches. Should the creeping barrage advance too far or too quickly ahead, it could actually leave the attackers terribly exposed – such as happened during the Battle of the Somme in 1916 and to the French at the Second Battle of the Aisne in April 1917, with appalling casualties by consequence. Yet eventually the British mastered creeping barrages of almost baroque complexity. During the Battle of Passchendaele, for example, one artillery battery had to perform no less than forty-five distinctive 'lifts' during the bombardment. In late-war actions, British troops might be no less than 100yds behind the impact zone of their own artillery (in some battle plans, Allied commanders allowed for a 10 per cent loss rate of troops to 'friendly fire'.) Note that creeping barrages could also be reversed in direction, ranging back over already pounded positions to hit the defenders as they emerged from the first firestorm.

By the time of the Battle of Cambrai, the artillery's potential as the true battlefield killer was being refined by another technological breakthrough. The core mathematical and practical challenge of indirect fire (artillery fire directed at a target the artillery crew cannot see) was that of getting the fire to fall accurately on to the intended target. For the early years of the war, this was largely achieved by 'registering' the guns on to the target before the main bombardment was delivered. Practically, this involved a single gun in a battery firing individual rounds towards the target. The impact of the rounds would be observed by either a ground-based forward observation officer (FOO) or by an FOO flying in a reconnaissance aircraft. The FOO would then communicate corrections in elevation and azimuth back to the gun crew until the fire was on target. At this point, the rest of the battery could be configured to fire at the same point.

Registering guns on a target was a laborious and tactically problematic method of artillery ranging. In short, it gave the game away, telling the enemy when and where a preparatory bombardment would come. Hence Britain's artillerymen set themselves the intellectual challenge of how to range guns on to a target without fire registration, thereby achieving complete surprise when the guns finally let fly.

By the time of the Battle of Cambrai, a new technique had emerged, known as 'map shooting'. As its name suggests, map shooting involved registering the guns on the target without actually firing, just taking co-ordinates from a map. Of course,

24. British gunner copying gun registrations. The Book of History, The World's Greatest War, Vol. XVII, The Grolier Society, New York, 1920. Courtesy of www.gwpda.org.uk

the important requirement here was accurate maps, something that was in desperately short supply at the beginning of the war. By 1917, however, the BEF's field survey companies had provided good-quality scale maps of the battle front, through which it was possible to plot both the position of the British gun batteries and their relationship to the enemy targets, and therefore calculate the bearing and elevation of the guns without actually firing ranging shots. Surprise, therefore, could be complete. Alongside map shooting, there were many other advances in artillery fire control. Techniques and technologies of 'flash spotting' and 'sound ranging', for example, provided the means of locating enemy gun batteries by visual (spotting the gun flash) and auditory means, making counter-battery fire that much more effective.

We should not, however, imagine that the Germans were simply passive targets beneath the muzzles of British guns. The crucible of combat experience had refined their defensive tactics to a sophistication never really achieved by their opponents. One of their key innovations was the 'elastic defence in depth' or

Eingreifentaktik ('intervention tactic'). Like the British, the German trenches had several parallel lines of defence, but the Germans often had their main line of defence set back from the forward frontline, which was frequently only lightly manned. Under attack, therefore, the German frontline would resist the assault but then often relinquish the positions, allowing the British, French or other troops to surge forward, stretching their logistics, communications and artillery support. Then the attackers would run up against several other German lines, plus counter-attacks and flanking artillery fire, and would lose the ground they had gained as the German defences flexed back into shape. Combined with excellent defensive positions, ones that locked attackers into terrifying crossfires and kill zones, the Germans would never be defeated by any single technology, no matter how persuasive.

25. German ordnance being moved into position and aligned for firing. The Illustrated War News, 12 April 1916.

Armour

We tend to forget now that the British led the way in terms of armoured warfare between 1914 and 1918. Prior to the First World War, and during its early years, the British Army gained experience with using armoured cars (in many cases actually little more than armour-plated civilian vehicles) in overseas policing and light expeditionary roles. This experience in turn led to the concept of more heavily armed and armoured vehicles, conceived particularly by assistant secretary to the Committee of Imperial Defence, Colonel Ernest Swinton. Swinton proposed vehicles capable of crossing battlefields while impervious to enemy small-arms fire, and providing close-range, mobile fire support at the very front of an attack or advance. Note that another envisaged purpose, one that would be crucial to the Battle of Cambrai, was that tanks could serve to grind a path through barbed-wire defences, to make gaps for the infantry to exploit. They also had to be capable of crossing trenches.

The organisation tasked with developing such vehicles was the 'Landships Committee', formed in February 1915 by First Lord

26. Armoured cars such as these began to prove their worth on the East African front. The Illustrated War News, 12 April 1916.

'TANK'

The semi-nautical term 'landship', when applied to heavy armoured vehicles, was eventually dropped in favour of 'tank', this being the title originally given to the British vehicles to hide their true identity from the Germans.

of the Admiralty Winston Churchill, under the auspices of the British Admiralty. The first crude tank prototypes emerged from the summer of 1915, boxy steel vehicles with the continuous-link tracks that would give them true cross-country mobility. These prototypes eventually led to the British Army's first production tank, the Mk I, by January 1916. Having a now-classic rhomboidal shape, with caterpillar tracks running around the length of its outer frame, the Mk I was a long way from the turreted tank shape with which we are familiar today. Powered by a 105hp Daimler-Knight six-cylinder engine, it weighed (depending on the variant) up to 28 tons and could only move at 4mph (much less over poor terrain). This lumbering beast was produced in two principal types, according to the armament configuration. The 'Male' tank was equipped with two 6pdr guns in sponsons on the hull sides, plus a secondary armament of four 0.303in Hotchkiss machine-guns. The 'Female' tank was armed with six machine-guns (four Vickers and two Lewis), to provide a light support option. The crew of both tanks was eight men.

Cambrai was not the first battle in which armour was committed on a significant scale. Vehicles of the Heavy Section, Machine Gun Corps – the tank's first official unit – were sent into action on the Somme on several occasions in the autumn of 1916, at Delville Wood then at Flers. Although the Germans were initially shocked by the confrontation, the combat results were not entirely positive. Mechanical breakdown plagued many of the vehicles, and they often became stuck in wide trenches. Moreover, conditions for the

27. An experimental transport tractor van, enabled to move in 'caterpillar fashion' due to the addition of tracks. Such vehicles as these were a precusor to the tank. The Illustrated War News, 19 April 1916.

crews inside almost defy description. Packed inside the bucketing iron box, the crew endured temperatures in excess of 100°F (38°C), poisoning from carbon monoxide and cordite fumes, deafening noises from engine and gunfire, and splinter injuries caused by bullets hitting the outer hull and shaking off fine metal shards (known as 'splash') from the interior metal. (For this latter reason, tank crews wore veils of chain-link metal over their faces.) Deployment during the Third Battle of Ypres in 1917 was even more disastrous – large numbers of tanks simply became bogged down in the mud, to become sitting ducks for enemy shellfire (a tank was easily demolished by a shell strike, particularly to the top of the hull).

Despite the unpromising start to the tank's career, there were still those who kept faith with the tank concept. The tank was mechanically improved, resulting in the Mk IV, the tank that would become the definitive model of both Cambrai and the First World War. Experience led to innovation. 'Fascines' – 15ft-diameter bundles of brushwood – were carried atop Mk IVs as trench-crossing devices; the bundle was rolled into a trench and the tank could then

GERMAN ARMOUR

The Germans, it should be noted, never embraced armour during the war in the same way as the British. Of its principal variety of the tank – the monstrous A7V – only twenty-one specimens were made during the entire war. Hence the Battle of Cambrai was never really a 'tank battle' as such, but purely a one-sided use of armour as mobile infantry support weapons.

28. The tank made famous by the Battle of Cambrai. This iconic image has come to represent the birth of tank warfare during the First World War. The Illustrated London News, 1 December 1917.

29. 'Crusty' crosses a shell-hole, although many tanks were to get bogged down in such obstacles during the battle. The Illustrated London News, 1 December 1917.

use it to cross a wide gap. Similarly, a long hardwood beam could be deployed as an 'undatching gear'; the beam could be linked to the tracks by chains and then used to gain purchase to pull the tank free of muddy ground or from a shell-hole. Tactically, many in the Tanks Corps – the new heavy armour formation created in July 1917 – also felt that the tank had not been used wisely, thrown into battle on unsuitable terrain with uncertain purpose.

At Cambrai, the tank would have a very clear objective. The actual tactical plan for the battle is discussed in the next chapter, but the tank's role as a scythe through barbed-wire defences was going to be critical at Cambrai. Descriptions of the barbed wire of the Hindenburg Line in 1917 speak with virtual reverence about the endless, twisting rivers of steel in front of the German trenches. Robert Woollcombe notes of the frontal aspect of the defences at Cambrai:

> Accounts vary of five, even six belts of wire. Third Army notes issued at the time stated that there were four belts of wire each some twelve yards in width with projecting triangles, forming a wired zone a hundred yards deep.
>
> Woollcombe, p.36

This was just the wire of the foremost 'Outpost Zone' – each subsequent line of resistance was equally wired. There was no way unsupported infantry could breach such defences on their own.

The tank, used in large numbers, offered a potential solution to this problem, especially under the combined-arms tank-infantry doctrine devised by Fuller. Under his system, three tanks (an armoured section) would be assigned to lead each infantry company in the attack. The tanks would push ahead in an arrow formation – an 'Advanced Tank' at the lead, with two 'Main Body Tanks' to the rear and either side. The infantry followed behind the two main body tanks, and were separated into four platoons: two 'trench-cleaning' platoons and two 'trench-stop' platoons. The advanced tank would grind a path through the barbed wire, using its tracks plus towed grappling hooks the size of anchors to crush or drag the wire out of the way, while also delivering suppressive fire on the enemy positions. The main body tanks would then push through the wire and cross the enemy trenches, before turning to provide assault support to the infantry attack, which had advanced through the wire gaps in single-file formations. (The advanced tank would at this point act as a reserve to the main body tanks.) Once through the wire, trench-cleaning platoons would attack the enemy trenches, using grenades and rifle fire to clean a trench section by section. The trench assault would be assisted by the tanks themselves, which delivered enfilading fire from their own guns. The trench-stop platoons would then consolidate a captured section of trench.

What we get at Cambrai, and what makes the battle so fascinating, is the clash between two sides at the cutting edge of tactical innovation. The British were pioneering new forms of combined-arms assault, while the Germans had perfected both the physical structure and tactical handling of a defence. Which side would win out would only be revealed in the battle itself.

THE DAYS BEFORE BATTLE

The month before the Cambrai offensive was launched was a hive of activity behind the British lines. Units were gathered and consolidated, training was undertaken and, most importantly, the actual attack plan was refined and shaped. The plan, unimaginatively codenamed 'Operation GY', had emerged by the end of the October 1917. Like many British battle plans of the First World War, its early stages were laid down with some precision, while its longer-term development was more ambiguous.

Operation GY

As explained above, responsibility for Operation GY fell to III and IV Corps, Third Army, plus the Tank Corps and the Cavalry Corps. V Corps was also to be involved, technically as a reserve but practically to consolidate ground secured by the cavalry exploitation. In total, the British were bringing nineteen infantry divisions, more than 400 tanks and 40,000 cavalrymen to the offensive.

The extent of the attack was actually quite limited, a front of some 6 miles from the Canal du Nord in the north to Bonavis to the south-east. The general tenor of the offensive was to crack the Hindenburg Line and drive out beyond to break the German lines of communication. The Hindenburg Line itself, however,

30. A French fire trench at Verdun. The Illustrated War News, 26 April 1916.

was a complicated entity. Looking north-east from the British frontline, the first line of defences was the Outpost Zone. This was not a continuous trench line, but rather a series of disconnected trenches and armed outposts, protected by substantial barbed-wire networks. A few hundred yards behind the Outpost Zone began the Hindenburg Line proper. Here was a major trench network, consisting of a fire trench and, some 200yds further back, a support trench, both heavily protected by barbed wire and by the infantry and machine-gunners. The trenches themselves measured about 7ft deep and up to 12ft wide, formidable obstacles for both men and tanks. Further back again was the Hindenburg Support Line, also composed of both fire trench and support trench, and equally formidable in defensive qualities. Behind this, roughly 4,000yds from the pre-offensive frontline, the Germans positioned many of their long-range howitzer batteries, which could provide fire support across the Cambrai sector. Further back still was another fire and support trench system, the Siegfried II, which, although less heavily wired than the more forward lines, still formed a powerful backstop to the Hindenburg Line. Taken together, the German defences at Cambrai were more than 5,000yds deep.

The opening element of Operation GY was to be a powerful and combined attack by tanks, infantry and artillery, delivered with complete surprise to the defenders. IV Corps was operating in the northern part of the front, while III Corps was to the south. The major objective of IV Corps was to punch through lines of German defence and capture the strategic high ground of Bourlon Ridge, a place from which the Germans were able to control their artillery. The need to take Bourlon Ridge, with its well-defended wood, as a Day 1 objective came from Haig himself, despite the fact that many senior commanders (including Byng) doubted the viability of such a goal. IV Corps was to advance through the Outpost Zone, Hindenburg Line and Hindenburg Support Line, taking Flesquières in the process, before even reaching the ridge; a tall order for any fighting force. III Corps, meanwhile, was to operate on the right flank of the advance, between the St Quentin canal and Bonavis. It was to push forward through the German defences and capture canal crossings at Marcoing and Masnières, forming a bridgehead and a gap in the German line through which the cavalry could drive through, raiding towards Walincourt and moving to the east of Cambrai to provide flank protection.

Although the battle that was about to take place took the name of Cambrai, the town itself was not actually a primary initial objective of the offensive. In fact, the thought of becoming embroiled in a difficult street battle meant that Haig and others preferred simply isolating the town and its garrison, and cutting off its communications with the rest of the front, then taking it later in the battle with cavalry, if viable.

In terms of the extended objectives of the offensive, here was some ambiguity. For a start, Haig had emphasised that if the offensive did not bear adequate fruit within the first forty-eight hours he would bring it to a halt, as beyond that time period the German defence would become virtually impenetrable as reinforcements reached the frontlines. The cavalry were to perform numerous exploitations into the German rear, taking key bridges along the Sensée River and St Quentin canal, and helping capture various villages such as Bourlon, Noyelles, Fontaine and Cantaing, and slight hills around Douai and the Scarpe, many of these gains to be consolidated by V Corps. The application of V Corps as an active component of the initial objectives meant that the British offensive at Cambrai effectively had little in the way of a true reserve force, a risky strategy given the German capabilities for counter-attacking. Yet once the initial objectives were taken, the broader objectives petered off into vague ideas. Woollcombe notes that 'Haig considered that advance guards of all arms might ultimately be pushed across the Sensée towards the scarpe east of Douai, with the main body of cavalry streaming to the north-east towards Valenciennes and the Belgian frontier' (Woollcombe, p.31). Nevertheless, such goals would only be considered opportunistically once the outcomes of the immediate two-day offensive had made themselves apparent.

Before looking at the physical preparations for the offensive, the planned deployment of tanks need to be explained. On the maps of the Cambrai offensive, the British delineated three lines, indicating progressive objectives for both infantry and cavalry. The first line, the 'Blue Line' (after the colour used on the map), incorporated the Outpost Zone and Hindenburg Line, plus Havrincourt and Ribécourt, while the 'Brown Line' took in Flesquières and the Hindenburg Support Line. Finally, the 'Red Line' incorporated the Siegfried II defences, and was also known to the British as the Masnières–Beaurevoir Line. Dedicated 'Wire Crushing Tanks', allocated on the basis of one three-tank section per infantry battalion, plus a second wave of 'Fighting Tanks' (eighteen to each brigade front), would take responsibility for the Blue Line objectives. In this wave there would be 216 tanks in

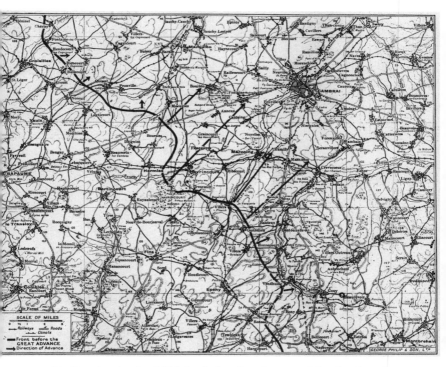

31. Map showing the British line before the advance and the direction of the advance. The Illustrated London News, 1 December 1917.

total, or one for every 100yds of frontline. Thereafter a third wave of ninety-six tanks plus infantry would push through the Blue Line and drive on to take the Brown Line objectives. From that point on, the Tank Corps was to advance and capture a variety of objectives in the German rear, while cavalry and infantry forces pressed on to the Red Line.

Interestingly, during the joint tank-infantry training described below, some divisions – specifically the 51st and 62nd – modified the tactics originally outlined by Fuller. In Fuller's original conception, the tanks of each section cross the fire trench at a common point (the fascine dropped by the advanced tank), while the modified tactic had the three tanks crossing at separate points before eventually coming together at a common crossing point on the support trench. Also, while Fuller recommended that the infantry behind the tanks advance in single file, the new plan saw one platoon following in four sections, set in line abreast formations, while the second platoon advanced in section columns. Such changes to the tank formations often did not go down well with the tank commanders, but the proof of the pudding would be in battle. The offensive was scheduled for 20 November 1917.

Preparations

Preparations for the Cambrai offensive began in earnest in early November, as vast amounts of men, armour, artillery and supplies began to organise themselves behind the frontline. The plan for unprecedented infantry-armour co-ordination meant that joint training had to be performed at a rapid pace. Such training took place at several locations in northern France, with each division theoretically allocated ten days of practical instruction alongside the armour. Opinions of the value of the training seem to vary according to the source. Some soldiers felt that it gave an invaluable integration between tank and infantry, while others were less convinced, such as tanker Second Lieutenant Horace Birks:

> Looking back on the exercises one realises how very simple and ineffective they were. In the circumstances, it was difficult to do more than practice very simple evolutions with the infantry.
>
> Quoted in Captain Geoffrey Dugdale, *'Langemarck' and 'Cambrai': A War Narrative 1914–1918*, Shrewsbury, Wilding & Son Ltd, 1932, p.96

Regardless of the quality of training, it does seem that many infantry, especially new recruits, were at least encouraged by the physical sight and presence of the tanks, although veterans who had witnessed or heard about tanks in action had more guarded morale.

Following training, there was the vexing logistical challenge of deploying more than 400 tanks to their offensive jumping-off points without alerting the Germans to their presence. The entire Tank Corps was transported by thirty-six trains to Bray-sur-Somme, then taken on to the frontline positions, with roughly twelve tanks transported on flat cars pulled by a single train. The logistical, scheduling and engineering challenges of this railway deployment were daunting, especially as the rail movements to the front were made during the night, to shield the tanks from the eyes of German reconnaissance aircraft. Once detrained, the tanks then used their own power to crawl to their forward then start positions. The actual campaign start line for the tanks was set some 1,000yds back from the German frontlines, so that the Germans could not hear engine noise as the tanks deployed into position. Once in place – a process that was performed on the night of 19 November – the tanks were covered with camouflage netting to hide their presence. (Each tank's position was designated by a sign displaying the tank's number.) Occasional machine-gun fire from the British lines was used to mask the sound of tank and vehicle engines.

The 1,000 British artillery pieces also had to be moved into position without alerting the enemy. Guns and ammunition choked the French roads at night, but by dawn they were in position and hidden under camouflaged material. At Havrincourt Wood, British soldiers even constructed, at night, a 2-mile long screen of foliage and brushwood along the edge of the wood, which shielded nearby artillery deployments from prying German eyes. On the night before the battle, smaller field artillery pieces were silently pulled forward into their supporting positions.

The infantry also moved up at night to ready themselves for the battle. Making this movement in the winter darkness tightened battle anxiety a little further. White tape was laid across the ground for units to follow to their designated trench and in places where the tapes had disappeared the track marks of the tanks provided some guidance. Even so, the movement was difficult and stumbling. Nor did the soldiers have the opportunity for rest once they did reach the trench lines. In fact, the forward trenches were packed with huge numbers of troops, well over the positions' usual capacities. Add the chilly and damp November night, and the result was that the British and Commonwealth troops had a mostly sleepless night before embarking on the attack the next morning. (Some formations had made three or four consecutive night marches before finally arriving at their start trenches.)

While the ground troops were preparing themselves for the land offensive, in the skies above the aircrew of the Royal Flying Corps (RFC) were also training hard. The Battle of Cambrai would see the full integration of air assets into the battle plan. In the run-up to the battle, reconnaissance aircraft with fighter protection made numerous flights over German lines, often coming face to face with new high-performance generations of German fighter aircraft, such as the Fokker D VII, as well as anti-aircraft fire. Reconnaissance was a traditional role for the RFC, but at Cambrai it would also deploy aircraft in the ground-attack role, which was still largely experimental at this time. Sopwith Camels and other aircraft types were fitted with light (20lb) cable-released bombs to racks beneath the wings, and the pilots practised for some two weeks dropping the bombs against point targets. Just before the offensive was launched, the pilots were then given specific targets to attack, ranging from frontline trenches to supply hubs and enemy airfields. The fusion of air, artillery, armour and infantry in one co-ordinated whole was to break new tactical ground and augur the combined-arms operations of the world war just over two decades later.

What is remarkable about this picture is that the Germans did not detect the build-up opposite them, at least not in any meaningful way. There were suspicions amongst the German high command that the British might be about to launch an offensive at some sector of the front, while acknowledging that the area around Cambrai was only weakly defended. On 18 November, furthermore, German raids around Havrincourt took several British soldiers prisoner. Under interrogation the British troops gave away little, but the Germans

PREPARING THE ATTACK

'The great numbers of tanks moving forward to their assaulting positions at midnight, the sound of their engines only partly drowned by the pre-arranged fire from Lewis and machine-guns, their unmistakable tortoise shape silhouetted by gun flash or Very light against the skyline, and only partly disguised by the fascines they carried, the rattle of innumerable guns moving forward down the newly metalled roads, the ceaseless snakes of infantry winding forward to their positions of assembly, and above all the gentle southerly breeze, blowing in the direction of the enemy, made discovery at any moment possible. But the enemy took no notice.'

Captain D. MacKenzie, *The 6th Gordons in France and Flanders* (Aberdeen, Rosemount Press, 1921)

gleaned enough to expect an attack around Havrincourt, and put their 54th Division on alert. (It was likely that the prisoners' ignorance of the broader offensive picture, rather than their determination to hide the truth, was one reason why the German suspicions weren't heightened.) Then an intercepted British radio message, which gave significance to 20 November, plus a general sense of increased British activity behind the lines, led the Germans to reinforce their *Gruppe Caudry* (XIII Corps) with an infantry regiment. Warning was given to both XIII Corps and XIV Reserve Corps (*Gruppe Arras*) further north to expect an attack at Havrincourt on 20 November. They even suspected that the British would deploy tanks in significant numbers, although the occasionally audible engines were often discounted as artillery tractors.

For all these glimmers of relevant intelligence, the scale and scope of the Cambrai offensive remained hidden from the Germans. That such a degree of secrecy was achieved is testimony to the careful planning of British tacticians and logisticians. Now it remained for the offensive to be unleashed.

THE BATTLEFIELD:
WHAT ACTUALLY HAPPENED?

The First Day

0620hrs	The British offensive at Cambrai begins, with a surprise artillery barrage across the front followed closely by armour and infantry assaults
c. 0730hrs	British forces approach and attack the fire trench of the Hindenburg Line. This line of resistance collapses over the next two hours
0930hrs	Blue Line objectives reached. Ribécourt is taken, with 500 prisoners. Attack on Flesquières by 51st Division begins
0955hrs	Main artillery barrage against the Brown Line objectives ceases. Second wave of tanks and infantry advance through
1030hrs	Havrincourt falls to the 62nd Division
1100–1230hrs	III Corps forces reach St Quentin canal, and secure crossings at Marcoing and Masnières. All Brown Line objectives have been taken, expect Flesquières, where the British armour suffers heavy losses

32. A high-explosive shell bursts over the German trench lines. The Illustrated War News, 10 May 1916.

Any German ignorance about the impending British offensive at Cambrai was utterly shattered at 0620hrs on the morning of 20 November 1917. One thousand British guns, ranged on to their targets without the usual giveaway preparatory bombardment, unleashed a storm of fire on the enemy positions and logistical network. The first shells were smoke types, shrouding the Hindenburg Line with thick wraiths of white smoke and shielding German eyes from what was heading their way. The gunners then quickly switched to high-explosive, thermite, shrapnel and incendiary shells, causing death and appalling injury. The high-explosive shells were fitted with the new No.106 instantaneous fuse, which exploded on immediate contact with the ground and so worked as a more efficient wire cutter than many previous shells. (Earlier shells tended to bury their way a good distance into the ground before exploding, meaning that the earth dissipated much of their explosive force.)

Even as the artillery shells began to erupt amongst the German lines, the tanks were already rumbling forward on the attack, with the dim dawn light beginning to spill over the battlefield. Co-ordination between the tanks and artillery was tight. The artillery was to 'lift' its fire in a series of jumps, staying several hundred

33. German soldier surrendering. The Illustrated London News, 1 December 1917.

yards ahead of the foremost tanks at all times. (The barrage also had the virtue of leaving large sections of ground untouched by shellfire, making them more suitable to the smooth passage of infantry and tanks.) The infantry followed in the wake of the tanks, and thankfully the first few minutes brought little in the way of a German counter-response. Such had been the surprise of the attack that the counter-artillery and machine-gun responses were minimal, and some eyewitnesses of the attack describe an almost leisurely progression across the battlefield by confident troops.

Soon both tanks and men were descending upon the shell-ravaged positions of the Outpost Zone and Hindenburg Line. (This did not happen simultaneously across the front, as the Hindenburg Line fire trench was further away from III Corps start lines than from those of IV Corps.) The tanks poured cannon and machine-gun fire along the length of trench sections and into strongpoints. The huge fascines and grinding tracks were almost as much a source of terror to the German infantry as the gunfire, and many German troops simply swarmed around the armoured vehicles, hands held high in an act of surrender.

Of course, the experience inside the tanks for the crews was far from pleasant. One tanker, Private George Brown of No. 24 Company, 'H' Battalion, remembered the brutal sensations of the initial advance:

34/35. 'The Perfect Lady' – here a tank makes easy work of crossing the trenches. The Illustrated London News, 1 December 1917.

At first we were just firing in the general direction of the enemy lines. Even at this early stage, the atmosphere inside the tank was beginning to get unpleasant: the fumes from the engine, the cordite fumes, the heat from the exhaust pipe, which was now red-hot. The noise was terrific: the rattle of the Lewis guns, the empty cartridge cases landing on the floor of the tank, and the driver banging onto the engine cover signalling to the secondary gearsmen.

'Some Reminscences of Cambrai and the German March
Offensive by 97218 Private George Brown', EM2007.591

Whatever the horrors inside the tanks, the fact remained that they were doing their job well. Not only had the shelling removed large sections of barbed wire by the time the infantry reached the enemy lines, but the wire-clearing tanks performed their job admirably. Soldiers saw huge thickets of barbed wire so dense 'that you could barely poke a broom handle through it' cleared down to dirt by the wire hooks hauled by the armour. The infantry discovered that all they needed to do was walk through the gaps in the wire and descend upon the German trenches.

The early morning hours brought a rush of victories along the length of the British front of attack. The precise times at which individual positions were taken are hard to ascertain, as there was often an interval between the time at which a trench or strongpoint fell and the moment the report reached headquarters. Times given in this account, therefore, should be taken as approximations in many instances.

The advance between 0700hrs and 0900hrs exceeded all British expectations. On the IV Corps front, the 62nd and 51st Divisions surged forward towards Havrincourt, assaulting German positions already rocked by a crushing bombardment. The Hindenburg Line directly in front of Havrincourt had been pounded by shells for thirty minutes, giving British troops time to cross the mile between their jumping off point and the line, plus defeat the Outpost Zone positions along the way. The 'Grand Ravine' defences in front of Havrincourt (so called on account of the depression they occupied), previously treated with respect by the British planners, was the scene of a rout, German soldiers fleeing from the battlefield and often abandoning their weapons in the process. Havrincourt village itself was a tougher nut to crack, and didn't succumb to the British until

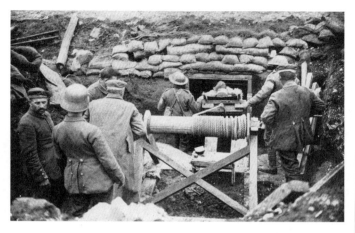

36/37. Makeshift dressing stations were created in deep dugouts to tend to the wounded. Here German prisoners can be seen helping the British to haul the wounded out of deep trench systems using a windlass. The Illustrated London News, 1 December 1917.

1030hrs. Snipers and machine-gunners in the village and Havrincourt chateau inflicted serious casualties on the 62nd Division. Only with close tank support was resistance within the village finally broken.

38. Tanks crossing a light railway before going into action at Cambrai. The Illustrated London News, 1 December 1917.

Meanwhile, by 0845hrs British tanks were crossing the Bapaume–Cambrai railway line that ran through the northern edge of Havrincourt. The collapse of the German front was now broadening. By 1000hrs, virtually all of the Blue Line objectives in IV Corps sector had been achieved, with the 10th Royal Inniskilling Fusiliers, acting without the support of tanks in the far north of the battle front, taking the German trenches on the east bank of the Canal du Nord, helping to secure the left flank of the British advance. Woollcombe notes that

> So successful was the attack here that by 9.15 a.m. over a thousand yards of the Hindenburg trench up the west bank of the canal had been captured, to a point even forward of the Brown Line.
>
> Woollcombe, p.76

Over on III Corps' front, similar progress was being made, with a notable exception to be discussed. By 0800hrs, the Hindenburg Line in front of Ribécourt had been reached and crossed by many elements of the corps. Within a further ninety minutes of action, Ribécourt itself had fallen to the British and most of the Blue Line objectives had been consolidated. The divisions pushed on towards the Brown Line. The artillery bombardment of these positions ceased at 0955hrs across the front (although smoke was delivered for another twenty-five minutes), by which time the second wave of tanks and infantry had pushed through the Blue Line and added additional impetus to the attack. The artillery had now fulfilled its overall bombardment plan for the opening phases of the Battle of Cambrai. It had served its purpose well, both in its co-ordination with the advancing tanks and infantry, and in its skilled demonstration of map shooting. Testimony from many British soldiers explains how many Germans were reduced to shattered, helpless figures by the intensity of the shelling, and could do little more than thrust their hands into the air in surrender when confronted by the grinding treads and rattling guns of the tanks.

III Corps now began its push towards the Siegfried II Line and its primary objectives of Marcoing and Masnières, driving along the Bonavis Ridge on its right flank. Progress was maintained at a good rate. By 1100hrs British tanks and 29th Division infantry were making penetrations of the St Quentin canal, fighting their way into Marcoing and Masnières. Yet as several hours had now elapsed since the beginning of the offensive, the German resistance was beginning to strengthen as the initial shock wore off. The British troops faced heavy small-arms fire, including from anti-tank rifles and machine-guns firing armour-piercing rounds, inflicting casualties on both infantry and armour. British tanks had to enter the urban environments and fire at point-blank range into the houses to secure routes for the infantry. Furthermore, the Germans had both bridges at Marcoing and Masnières wired for demolition, and their loss would be a serious blow to the subsequent British advance. The Germans had already made some tactical demolitions at other parts of the front. For example, in the early hours of the battle they had blown the Bapaume–Cambrai road bridge that ran over the Canal du Nord, an act that would seriously impair IV Corps' logistics during the remainder of the offensive.

The resistance intensified in both Marcoing and Masnières. At the former, eight tanks from 'A' Battalion managed to prevent the Germans from destroying the bridge. More tanks from 'B' Battalion arrived at 1130hrs, but the tanks had scant infantry support at this time and could do little more than hold their end of the bridge. Crossings were found for the 29th Division infantry elsewhere, however, and they pushed across the canal to link up with elements of the Newfoundland Regiment that had already made crossings at Masnières. For the tanks, the Masnières road bridge capture had proved to be a trying ordeal. The Germans succeeded in damaging the bridge with a demolition charge, and one tank – *Flying Fox II* of 'F' Battalion – brought it crashing down when it attempted a tentative crossing. The infantry had better luck, as the 2nd Hampshire Regiment and parts of the Newfoundland Regiment found other bridges and crossings. They pushed across the canal and by the early afternoon the British forces were making some limited assaults against positions of the Siegfried II Line. Note that on the British side of the canal some Siegfried II positions were already secured, such as at Nine Wood and Noyelles.

The First Morning

Worrying signs – Flesquières

The first morning of the Battle of Cambrai was one of undoubted success for the British. An advance of more than 4,000yds had been made, and virtually all of the Blue and Brown Line objectives had been taken, leaving the rest of the day for a rapid exploitation. Yet we must be cautious about overplaying the victories of this day. Certainly, the Germans as a whole were utterly dominated by the combined-arms tactics, but as they began to show signs of recovery, the British had to fight hard for their gains.

For a start, tanks were being lost in significant quantities. Many of these losses were due to mechanical failure (around seventy-one vehicles), tanks simply grinding to a halt through broken tracks, blown engines and failed transmissions, amongst other problems. Another forty-three vehicles had become 'ditched' and were abandoned. The day also saw the loss of sixty-five tanks to enemy action, a troubling rate of destruction. Most of these losses came when German artillery crews managed to bring their guns to bear on the lumbering armoured vehicles. For example, the 20th Division's attack towards the 'Welsh Ridge' defences in III Corps sector saw the tank crews of 'I' Battalion up against German field guns, as Second Lieutenant George Parsons remembered in an account written after the war:

> I saw two Germans ahead of us with a tripod machine-gun but they vanished before we could open fire. Then we were hit. The first shell hit the fascine and left track and I remember the acrid cordite smell. I tried to move the tank, but we were without traction. Then the second shell hit us on the left side and that was it. I got out and tried to hide in a very shallow shell hole, but abandoned that for a nearby trench, and in that got back some 200 yards to our advancing infantry.
>
> IWM PP/MCR/100, J.K. Wilson Papers, Parsons to 'Jake' Wilson
> (January 1969)

As Parsons' account demonstrates, once a tank was a 'disability kill' (meaning that it could not be moved), it was then a sitting duck to be finished off. The Mk IV's maximum armour depth was 0.47in, which was fine for seeing off small-arms fire but presented almost no protection against a direct hit from an artillery shell, even a common high-explosive shell.

The destruction of tanks by artillery was repeated up and down the front, but nowhere more worryingly than during the 51st Division's assault upon Flesquières Ridge, sitting north-east of Havrincourt and almost in the centre of the British front. Although positions either side of Flesquières were taken by the British advance, Flesquières itself remained obdurately in the hands of the Germans, including the 108th Field Artillery Regiment, which had already gained some experience (against the French) and training in delivering anti-tank fire. It totalled nine batteries of guns – three field howitzer batteries, six field-gun batteries and five heavy batteries.

The German positions at Flesquières had been pounded by both artillery and British air attacks, inflicting heavy casualties but not putting all of the artillery pieces out of action. Furthermore, the elevated terrain favoured the defenders, who were emplaced in strong positions on the reverse slope of the ridge. The British tanks, who in their advance up the ridge would eventually present themselves in silhouette to the German gunners, effectively rode into a killing zone.

The British assault on Flesquières began at around 0930hrs, and quickly the German gunners turned their muzzles on the slow-moving targets. Tanks were torn apart by the heavy shells, their light armour blasted open and thrown across the battlefield. Soon German gunners began to achieve impressive kill rates. Two batteries alone accounted for six tanks within a few minutes. Most famously, a single German officer reputedly manned a gun and destroyed no less than sixteen British tanks before he was finally killed. Such was the reputation of this gunner that even Douglas Haig's Cambrai dispatch acknowledged the bravery of the officer, which 'aroused the admiration of all ranks'. There is some ambiguity about this story, however, not least of which is the fact that the Germans themselves did not single out one individual above all others for praise following the engagement. Many other tanks were also destroyed by resourceful German infantry, using grenades and armour-piercing bullets.

Whatever the truth of the 'Flesquières gunner', there was certainly no denying that Flesquières Ridge and the approaches to the village were soon littered with burning and wrecked tanks.

In such circumstances, the finely tuned ideas of tank-infantry co-operation broke down, and the advance in front of Flesquières ground to a halt. Much subsequent criticism for the failure to secure Flesquières, in fact, was directed at the General Officer Commanding (GOC) of the 51st Division, Major General Montague Harper. Harper was a powerful character who was not convinced of the tactical innovations proposed by the Cambrai battle plan. As already noted, the 51st Division modified Fuller's tank tactics, and at Flesquières Harper's further innovations came terribly unstuck. He positioned the infantry much too far behind the tanks (up to 400yds) to provide effective and immediate support, and also strung the infantry out in extended order rather than single file, which resulted in delays passing through the wire. Flesquières was certainly a worrying development for the overall battle plan, as a prominent German salient was now bulging out into the British line of advance.

Despite what had happened at Flesquières, in the III Corps' sector there at least seemed the possibility of a cavalry exploitation through the Marcoing–Masnières gap. Indeed, the Cavalry Corps had been on the move in force since the early hours of the campaign. The plan was for the 5th Cavalry Division to isolate Cambrai while the 2nd Cavalry Division turned south-east to protect the eastern flank of the offensive. The 3rd and 4th Cavalry Divisions could act as reserve forces to push deeper into German-occupied territory, if the situation allowed. The cavalry formed into two major lines of advance: one running from Viller Plouich to Marcoing, and the other from Les Rue Vertes (just west of Masnières on the St Quentin canal) back to Gouzeaucourt. By the time the cavalry were ready to make exploitations across the canal, however, the light was beginning to drain out from the winter day. 'B' Squadron of the Fort Garry Horse crossed the canal at Masnières and made a gallant assault on an enemy artillery battery, but as darkness fell most of the cavalry had to bed down for the night on the east side of the canal.

Taking Stock

There was no denying that the Germans had experienced a disastrous day in battle on 20 November 1917. The commander of the German Army Group North, Kronzprinz Rupprecht of Bavaria, had seen the near-total collapse of a 6-mile section of the Hindenburg Line, with British forces now pushing up against the rearmost Siegfried II positions. *Gruppe Caudry* had been routed, but Rupprecht and von der Marwitz still had fight in them yet. The priority was to reinforce the front immediately, in preparation for the certain continuation of the offensive the next day. The neighbouring army groups – *Arras* and *Quentin* – contributed six infantry battalions during the night. The 107th Division also added its weight to the German defences. This division was a veteran formation that had been fighting for the last two years on the Eastern Front. It had been redeployed to the Western Front on 18 November, fortuitously for *Gruppe Caudry*.

At home, the British people were excited by the news from the Western Front. For the cost of only 4,000 casualties (light by the standards of the time), the British and Commonwealth troops had literally pushed forward thousands of yards – nearly 5 miles at the advance's maximum extent. (Woollcombe points out that the similar gains of the Battle of Arras had cost the British 159,000 casualties.) They had secured most of their objectives up to the Red Line. The bells rang in jubilation, and the tactics of the offensive seemed thoroughly vindicated.

The British commanders faced the next day with some concern, however. The Tank Corps, the instrument that had been so vital in the day's victories, had been massively depleted during the fighting – 55 per cent of its tanks had been lost in just one day. The experience at Flesquières had shown that the Germans were not always intimidated by the presence of armour, particularly if that armour became separated from its infantry support.

39. *English Eastern county troops stop for a meal on a section of the Hindenburg Line. The Illustrated London News, 1 December 1917.*

Flesquières stood as a deep thorn in the British side at the end of Day 1, not least because it protected one of the approach routes to Bourlon Ridge, an objective that was also meant to fall on the first day of battle. The problem of what to do about Flesquières was nevertheless resolved during the night of 20/21 November. The German commander at Flesquières, a Major Krebs, was hoping for reinforcements if he was to defend his salient against flanking attacks the following day. When it became apparent that these would not be forthcoming, he pulled back from Flesquières to more defensible positions to the north at Cantaing and Fontaine.

Yet even this development, revealed by a late-night reconnaissance patrol of Highlanders, did not give Haig and the British commanders complete peace of mind. The Germans were known for their powers of recovery, and with every passing hour the defences would strengthen and more troops would be channelled to the front, building the possibility of a future counter-attack. By contrast, the British and Commonwealth soldiers were generally shattered by sleep deprivation and combat, and their morale was further diminished by a night out in the open for most, under chilly November rain. Some faced an even worse night: soldiers of the Hampshires and Worcestershires were involved in heavy night fighting in Masnières. There were also issues of logistics – the roads forward to the front were in many places packed with refugees and also drawing the attention of German long-range artillery, all of which hampered the smooth flow of supplies up to the front.

Haig and Byng now had to re-evaluate their plan, in readiness for the offensive to continue the next day. Essentially, the overall objectives were not modified; such would scarcely be practical anyway, given the late hour and the difficulties of transmitting radically revised plans amongst so many units. The surviving tanks were reallocated amongst the formations, with II Brigade being moved over to IV Corps, which would secure Flesquières at dawn

40. Pioneer units were used to help clear the way for artillery and transport. The Illustrated London News, 1 December 1917.

41. Blocked roads were a major problem in hampering the advance, here trees felled by the Germans obstruct a main road. The Illustrated London News, 1 December 1917.

42. Refugees from Cantaing flood the roads around the area, halting the Allied advances. The Illustrated London News, 1 December 1917.

before making a general thrust forward at 1000hrs. An hour later, III Corps would resume the attack out from Masnières. Given that Haig had initially given the Cambrai offensive forty-eight hours to clinch its results, a lot was riding on the next day's action.

Pushing On

| 21 November | 0300hrs | Germans have pulled out of Flesquières to more defensible positions to the north at Cantaing and Fontaine |
| | 0630hrs | The German 107th Division makes a limited counter-attack around Noyelles |

21 November	**1030hrs**	The British make several assaults on the Siegfried II Line. Cantaing and Fontaine are taken
	1320hrs	11th King's Royal Rifle Corps (KRRC) makes an unsuccessful attempt to secure crossings of the St Quentin canal at Crévecoeur
	1400–1430hrs	The 87th Brigade and the 88th Brigade attack out from positions at Marcoing and Masnières
	1600hrs	The British take Noyelles, defeating the German 1st Battalion, 232nd Regiment, 107th Division
22 November	**0700hrs**	The 185th Brigade faces a counter-attack by the 386th *Landwehr* Regiment and the 50th Regiment
	1000hrs	German forces launch counter-attack against Fontaine
	1430hrs	Fontaine is captured by the German 46th Regiment
	Evening	62nd Division is replaced in the line by the 40th Division

The III Corps' operation to take the Siegfried II Line opposite Marcoing and Masnières experienced an early shock at 1030hrs on the morning of 21 November. Even by 0630hrs, the Germans had been demonstrating tenacious defence, when the 10th Battalion, 59th Brigade (10th/59th Brigade) was prevented from crossing a canal bridge around Crévecoeur. Then four hours later the German 107th Division actually made a limited counter-attack around Noyelles. The attack was stopped from making significant progress by virtue of RFA bombardment and a hastily improvised defence at Nine Wood, and later in the day a scratch force of lancers and fusiliers drove the Germans out of the village.

The fact was that the momentum was beginning to bleed out of the British advance. Both the 59th and the 87th Brigades made assaults against the Siegfield II Line during the morning, operating

43. The original caption for this image of German prisoners at Cambrai read: 'like a ridge of Kipling's "whale-backed downs": a slag-heap captured, recaptured, and again captured – German prisoners passing by.' The Illustrated London News, 1 December 1917.

with limited tank support. The German defenders turned back many attacks with vigour, aided by the issue of anti-tank small-arms ammunition that in one case put 100 holes in a single British tank. IV Corps was also experiencing its fair share of tribulations. The initial morning operation, to clear Cantaing, was successful. It included a mounted cavalry attack by the 2nd Dragoon Guards, one of whom (Private Chris Knight) described something of the melee:

> Donnelly, the Irishman, went raving mad, cutting and thrusting at the retreating Germans. Germans emerged from dugouts in all directions, some giving themselves up, others making a fight of it with a few bombs. No. 1 troop received the bombs in its midst. The bomb-throwers were accounted for with rifle and revolver. We took many prisoners, but the major portion of the garrison had cleared out before we arrived. Very soon their machine-guns were in action again, and shells were dropping in and behind the village.

> C.B. Purdom (ed.), *Everyman at War* (J.M. Dent, London, 1930) p.162

Cantaing fell to the British troops, and Fontaine was then taken by a tank-supported assault from the 7th Argyll and Sutherland Highlanders, and the 4th Seaforth Highlanders. Bourlon and Bourlon Wood were now flanked by the British from the east, but the attempts by the 62nd Division to attack Bourlon from the west were fought back by a trenchant defence. The effect of this localised defeat was that the Highlanders in Fontaine were left isolated, and at 1000hrs on 22 November they were attacked by a strong force of 1st and 2nd Battalions of the 46th Regiment. The Scots resisted with the determination for which they are famed, but they were heavily outnumbered and were eventually compelled to abandon Fontaine at 1430hrs, having suffered 319 casualties. To round off a testing day for the British, the 62nd Division were also counter-attacked and lost much of the territory they had captured the previous day. German forces now included the 50th Regiment, fresh to the battlefield. British forces were also in need of new blood, and the exhausted 62nd Division was replaced by the 40th Division on the evening of the 22nd.

Bourlon Wood

23 November	1030hrs	The British 40th and 51st Divisions launch a combined-arms assault against the German positions at Fontaine, Moeuvres, Bourlon Wood and Bourlon Village
	1130hrs	British tanks ('B' and 'C' Battalions) penetrate Fontaine, but are thrown out by a proficient anti-tank defence
	1200hrs	Royal Welch Fusiliers penetrate to the northern edge of Bourlon Wood
	1500hrs	German counter-attacks in Bourlon Wood push the lead elements of the 40th Division back to defensive positions deeper within the wood

44. *Highland Territorials during their advance after the taking of the German first line. The* Illustrated London News, *1 December 1917.*

45. *The Highlanders using duckboards to cross over a deep German fire trench. The* Illustrated London News, *1 December 1917.*

23 November	**1700hrs**	The attempt to capture Bourlon village fails, and the left flank of the 40th Division falls back to positions about 500yds south of the Bourlon
	c. 0000hrs	Both sides receive reinforcements during the night
24 November	**1530hrs**	14th Highland Light Infantry attack Bourlon, with elements reaching the far end of the village
	1600hrs	A German counter-attack at Bourlon Wood leaves the Highlanders in Bourlon trapped

The fighting of 22 November was a critical time for the British commanders. Haig was faced with the reality that his forty-eight-hour deadline had now passed, and all the intended objectives had not been taken. Furthermore, the counter-attacks and local defeats were indications that the German reinforcements were building up in strength and confidence.

Haig opted to continue the general offensive on the 23rd, during which he hoped to take Bourlon Wood, an objective that would shift the balance of power on the battle front in favour of the British. Byng and others concurred, as going on the offensive meant avoiding the difficulties of establishing a firm defensive line and relinquishing ground already taken.

The battle plan for 23 November was as ambitious as forces allowed, including major artillery resources (432 guns, five divisions' worth) and a total of eighty-eight tanks. The attack would take place across all 6 miles of front, but the chief objective was Bourlon Wood. While the 51st Division would assault Fontaine and Moeuvres, against the forces of *Gruppe Caudry*, the 40th Division would launch the 199th Brigade against Bourlon Wood and the 121st Brigade against Bourlon village. They would be tackling Generalleutnant von Moser's *Gruppe Arras*, three divisions strong and with support from a fourth guards division.

The Germans had 200 artillery pieces and several squadrons of aircraft acting in support. It was not going to be an easy day.

At 1030hrs, the combined offensive was unleashed, imitating the first day of the campaign but this time without the advantage of German ignorance. Fontaine was an immediate setback. Although the village was struck heavily by British shells, the Germans slaughtered ranks of infantry with heavy machine-gun and artillery fire. Consequently, the British push in this sector stuttered to a halt, the attackers forced to dig in about 500yds short of the village itself. The nineteen supporting tanks made better initial progress, but were massacred at close range in the village by fire from a German truck-mounted anti-aircraft battery. Only six tanks made it back to their lines.

To the left of Fontaine, the attack against Bourlon Ridge was under way. A mixed force of Seaforth Highlanders and Argyll and Sutherland Highlanders probed into the easternmost extremities of Bourlon Wood, while to their left four battalions of Welsh troops, part of the 40th Division, drove headlong into the defences of the wood itself. The wood was a claustrophobic place in which to fight. In addition to the dense trees, which made linear movement impossible and reduced the light levels, the Germans had laced the terrain with bunkers, trenches, machine-gun nests and many other hazards. Combat took place at close quarters, even as the bullets and shells smashed through the trees above. Something of the nature of the fighting for the wood comes across in the 40th Division's official history:

> The din of battle within the wood was awe-inspiring. In front trees were falling wholesale from the shells of our guns, while around and behind the German projectiles were crashing everywhere. The roar was supplemented by the ceaseless chatter of enemy machine-guns and of our own Lewis guns …

Doggedly, the Welsh troops bombed, shot and cut their way through the wood over several hours, reaching the northern edge

46. A Highlander bringing in two captured German machine-gunners. The Illustrated London News, 1 December 1917.

of the wood by mid-afternoon. At the same time, the 12th Suffolks, 20th Middlesex and 13th Green Howards were striking towards Bourlon village itself, further to the west. This attack became bloody and problematic, not least because a push by the 36th Division on their left flank had failed, meaning that the advance on Bourlon was exposed to enfilading fire. Bourlon was momentarily penetrated by soldiers of the 13th Green Howards and the 12th South Wales Borderers, plus a handful of tanks, but the Germans pushed them out to the village's southern perimeter. At Moeuvres, Irish troops captured much of the village against fierce resistance, but then lost most of it during subsequent German counter-attacks. Having taken the German forward line, the British were finding the rearmost positions far more difficult. At 1500hrs, two regiments of Germans launched themselves against the Welsh troops in Bourlon Wood. In exceptionally brutal fighting, the Welsh were pushed back into the wood, but managed to dig in and hold a defensive line, reinforced by the 120th Division on the night of 23/24 November. Similarly, the Germans at Bourlon Wood were bolstered by the arrival of the

Guards Fusilier Regiment and two battalions of the 46th Reserve Infantry Regiment.

The day ended with a grim death toll on both sides, and neither Bourlon village nor its neighbouring wood were in British hands. Corpses littered woodland, hill and copse, shattered by shellfire, bullet and grenade. The offensive was certainly slowing, but fighting would continue to rage for several days yet. On 24 November, the British efforts focused on another attempted capture of Bourlon village, to be attempted by the 121st Brigade, strengthened by the 1st and 2nd Cavalry Battalions of the 40th Division, plus twelve tanks. Yet the Bourlon sector was now swelling with German reinforcements, and they showed their strength when the 9th Grenadier Regiment made a localised spoiling attack at dawn against the 119th Brigade in Bourlon Wood. Now the British showed their stubbornness in defence. They remained defiant and in position, hewing down German attackers with rifle and machine-gun fire and by 1615hrs had forced the Germans from the northern edge of Bourlon Wood.

Despite the heroic defence, it was apparent that the advantage was passing to the Germans. The commander of IV Corps, Lieutenant General Woollcombe, postponed an early morning attack against Bourlon village by 121st Brigade, but a failed order meant that the attack forged ahead and was roughly handled. Of the twelve tanks of 'I' Battalion that entered the village, eight were destroyed – the Germans were now getting the measure of tackling British armour. Highland infantry units made decent initial progress, but a company of 14th Highland Light Infantry (HLI) was separated and cut off in the south-east of the village. The centre of the village remained in German hands.

By 25 November, five days since the beginning of the Cambrai offensive, Haig's frustration was mounting. Not only did Bourlon remain out of reach, but the intended cavalry exploitation had not occurred. These failures took place against the backdrop of growing German strength in the sector and there was an evident sense that the Germans were preparing for a general counter-attack.

47. Irish troops rest alongside north-county units and the Scottish Territorials. The Illustrated London News, 1 December 1917.

48. Irish troops in action, crossing the German second line. The Illustrated London News, 1 December 1917.

Compounding the British maladies, the weather was steadily worsening – it began to snow on the evening of the 26th – and given recent experience at Ypres everyone knew what a problem the weather could become.

In many ways, it must have been obvious that the Cambrai push had had its day, not least because the British were even feeding recently relieved soldiers back into the line, despite their exhaustion. The one glimmer of light from the front was that the commander of the 19th Royal Welch Fusiliers, Lieutenant Colonel James Plunkett, was still leading a resolute defence of Bourlon Wood, one against which the waves of German attack were repeatedly breaking. The commander of the German 3rd Guards Division, Generalleutnant von Lindequist, even transmitted a signal on 24 November that declared, 'In spite of all our efforts, the British forces cannot be pushed out of the wood'.

The next morning brought an attempt by the 13th East Surreys to rescue the beleaguered Highland Infantry in Bourlon. Despite making some contact with the Highlanders' HQ, and fighting their way through the village without tank support, the East Surreys were eventually forced back, and at 0930hrs the eighty surviving men of the 14th Highland Light Infantry finally succumbed to the inevitable and surrendered to the Germans. At the back end of the afternoon, the 119th, 120th and 121st Brigades at Bourlon were relieved by the 186th and 187th Brigades of the 62nd (West Riding) Division.

One Last Push

25 November		
	0615hrs	The 13th East Surreys launch a relief operation for the Highland Light Infantry in Bourlon. It makes partial contact with the HLI, but is eventually forced back
	0930hrs	The surviving HLI troops in Bourlon surrender
	1600hrs	119th, 120th and 121st Brigades at Bourlon are relieved by the 186th and 187th Brigades of the 62nd (West Riding) Division

26 Nov		Both sides continue to exchange artillery and small-arms fire, but there is little change of position on the ground
27 November	**0620hrs**	British forces (1st Coldstream Guards and 3rd Grenadier Guards) launch another attempt to take Bourlon Wood and Fontaine
	1000hrs	The attack on Fontaine fails with heavy British casualties, and the troops there withdraw. German counter-attacks in Bourlon Wood also stop British ambitions there
	1030hrs	Assaults on Bourlon result in the separation of two battalions of 187th Brigade, which are forced back
	1500hrs	186th Brigade stops German counter-attacks around Bourlon

Despite all that was going against the British, Haig decided to authorise one last onslaught, in a nervy attempt to break out finally through Bourlon and consolidate some serious strategic gains. Haig was under some pressure from the government back home. Given the depredations of Ypres, the government was sensitive about major losses in manpower, and about the Cambrai battle devolving into an expensive exercise in attrition. Haig gambled on a final attack on 27 November, the plan being for the 62nd Division to take Bourlon while the Guards Division assaulted Fontaine. By this stage of the battle, many of the senior commanders had lost confidence in the overall value of continuing. The commander of the Guards Division, Major General Feilding, for example, felt that his now understrength division, supported by just twelve tanks, was simply not up to the task of taking Fontaine, which was bristling with Germans and heavily covered by artillery. He recommended instead retreating to a defensive line on the Flesquières Ridge, and sitting out the winter. At one point he said to Woollcombe, 'We shall do our best sir, but you ask a lot of us.'

ARTILLERY CASUALTIES

During the First World War, artillery came to inflict the majority of all casualties. British calculations put the figures at 59 per cent of all casualties, but French and German calculations even took the total as high as 89 per cent.

Throughout 26 November, the British artillery kept up a steady stream of punishment arcing through the cold winter air on to the German lines. Preparations for the actual attack, however, were perfunctory. In fact, many units did not receive their full orders until only twelve hours before the launch. Worse still, the dusting of snow turned into near-blizzard conditions.

At 0620hrs on 27 November, the assault was launched by freezing, bone-tired men. Some 350 British guns lay down a creeping barrage as cover, behind which the few tanks available ground forward towards their objectives. There was a disaster in the making. At Fontaine, once again British tanks made their way into the village, but were hunted by German tank-killing infantry squads, and the few surviving tanks were forced to retreat. Major Philip Hammond, No.18 Company, 'F' Battalion, Tank Corps, remembered the confusion of the street battle:

It was all badly and hurriedly thought out and we had not near enough infantry, though those we had were the best infantry in the world. The machine-gun fire from the right toward La Folie was simply terrific and cut up the Guards badly. Anyway we got all the tanks into the town and then indeed pandemonium broke loose. The Boche shelling was very heavy even in the west outskirts of the town itself, and our half-baked barrage was poor. The houses were full of Boches and we went down the streets firing into the houses till the infantry could rush in and bayonet them.

Letter from P. Hammond, 9 December 1917

49. German prisoners are used as stretcher-bearers, carrying a wounded British officer to a first aid post. The Illustrated London News, 1 December 1917.

For the infantry, the experience was even more appalling. As the quotation from Hammond above testifies, hundreds of troops were machine-gunned from La Folie Wood as they moved against Fontaine into the attack; at one point two companies of the 3rd Grenadiers were killed near the Cambrai–Bapaume road. The ferocity of the resistance from Fontaine meant the attack was doomed to fail from the outset. Indeed, by 1000hrs those who had survived the attack pulled back to their start positions, shocked and bloodied.

There was no encouragement from the assault on Bourlon either. The village was assaulted by the 186th and 187th Brigades, each coming at the objective from different angles. When the tanks pushed into the streets, they were hit by murderous fire from German assault guns and infantry armed with hefty demolition charges. Fourteen of the tanks were destroyed in total. The infantry also entered the village and engaged in hard fighting at close quarters with gun, bayonet and grenade. The German forces were soon counter-attacking across the front, and the British formations in the village became fragmented and outmanoeuvred. Although the German counter-attack was stopped by the 186th Brigade, the assault against Bourlon had clearly failed, with much cost. Haig ordered the offensive to cease and pushed three new divisions up into the line to hold back the Germans. From here, exhausted in the winter snow, the British forces at Cambrai would go no further.

Retaliation

30 November	0600hrs	Two German army groups launch a massive counter-offensive across the eastern side of the Cambrai front, aiming to reclaim all ground lost to the British
	0900hrs	*Gruppe Arras* begins its contribution to the counter-offensive along the Canal du Nord axis
	Morning	German advances towards Gouzeaucourt push the British back 3 miles, but a counter-attack retakes the village and establishes a new defensive line. Advances in other parts of the front are held back by British defenders, with minimal losses of ground
	Afternoon	Fighting continues throughout the afternoon
1 December	c. 0650hrs	Third Army launches its own counter-attack against the German offensive
	0715hrs	The Ambala Brigade, 5th Cavalry Division, plus the Guards Division assault at Gonnelieu and Gauche Wood
	0935hrs	The Mhow Brigade cavalry, with the 2nd Lancers in the forefront, begin an ultimately unsuccessful attack on Villers-Guislan

Afternoon   Fighting continues intensively at many points of the front, particularly at La Vacquerie, Les Rues Vertes, Masnières and on the St Quentin canal

Even as the British were fighting their final offensive of the Cambrai campaign, the Germans were preparing a major counter-offensive of their own. General Erich von Ludendorff (effectively the commander of all German forces), Rupprecht and von der Marwitz, plus other German Army commanders, were in conference on 27 November at La Cateau. There must have been some degree of confidence in the room. British exhaustion was evident, but by contrast the Germans had received no less than seven new infantry divisions into the sector, forming two new *Gruppen* in the process: *Gruppe Lewarde* to the north of *Gruppe Arras*, and *Gruppe Busigny* on the left flank of *Gruppe Caudry*. Furthermore, the Germans now had a total of 1,200 artillery pieces available, more than the British began the original offensive with. (The British would have been uncomfortably aware of the presence of German artillery resources, as the Germans began registering their guns on the enemy lines from the 28th.)

A clear plan emerged. After a short but very intense thirty-minute artillery bombardment, the attack would be delivered with three major thrusts, designed to cut off the salient created by the British gains. In the south, *Gruppe Busigny* was to strike across a broad front from south of Banteux to Vendhuile, pushing towards Gouzeaucourt. Further north, *Gruppe Caudry* would move against Flesquières, Havrincourt and Metz. To the west of Bourlon, meanwhile, *Gruppe Arras* would drive along the Canal du Nord, meeting up with *Gruppe Caudry* as the latter moved north from Havrincourt. One notable aspect of the German attack at Cambrai was to be application of *Stoßtruppen* tactics at the infantry level. In this operational model, the initial assault waves, armed with light machine-guns and flamethrowers, would move quickly and bypass key enemy points of defence, leaving them isolated to the rear to be mopped up by the second wave of the advance.

From 28–30 November, the Germans were in preparation for the offensive, gathering together their forces and distributing orders. They also engaged in some acts of deception, to wrong-foot the defenders. For example, on 28–29 November, *Gruppe Arras* bombarded Bourlon Wood with gas shells, putting the troops there in a state of readiness for an attack, even though this would not be a primary axis of the German offensive. However, the general British expectations of a major German counter-attack were limited and contemporary accounts of this pre-offensive period often speak of a general complacency in headquarters.

Any complacency was lost at 0600hrs on 30 November, when the German artillery hammer came crashing down on the British lines. When the barrage lifted, the German infantry swarmed through the early morning mist and the shell smoke as the British lines descended into chaos and confusion. Shelling cut many of the telephone lines between frontline units and the rear headquarters, making the co-ordination of a response across the front almost impossible. To prevent complete collapse, many British divisional commanders were forced to throw together ad hoc combat units from rear-echelon personnel. Gunners around Gonnelieu and Viller-Guislan fired against the advancing Germans until the enemy infantry were almost upon them, at which point they disabled their artillery and fought on with small arms.

Lieutenant John Lomax, an RFA officer of the 55th Division, experienced the confusion of combat and a violent descent into captivity when he fought in a quarry position under the full force of the German attack:

> We had been scattered and the scene was utterly unexpected and bewildering. Retreat never entered my head. With one of the rifles I was firing at anything that moved to the flanks when I spotted a German taking aim at me: he actually fired before I could get my gun up and his bullet went through my collar, drilling a neat hole

in and out but not touching me. At some time another German from the quarry lip must have dropped a bomb from above. The explosion knocked me over and for a spell I lay stunned in the dust. When I recovered my wits and tried to rise there was a German NCO standing over me with a massive pistol pointed at my head and, with a furious roar of words, he waved me back to where a soldier was standing guard over a few of my men.

John Lomax, IWM 88/27/1

British shock was nevertheless balanced by an aggressive defence, which was the undeniable equal to that of the Germans. The boldest German advances were made towards Gouzeaucourt, driving the British back up to 3 miles from their previous positions and taking the town. The 1st Brigade of the Guards Division was deployed at speed to Gouzeaucourt, while in the far south of the front the Cavalry Corps assisted VII Corps in an attack against the German southern flank. In a display of bravery and bold decision, Gouzeaucourt was recaptured and the British forces set up defensive positions to the east of the town, parallel to the railway line running north. Against what seemed to be total collapse, the British here had restored the line.

A similar story played out on other parts of the front. The 36th and 37th Brigades opposing *Gruppe Caudry*'s advance towards Metz were initially powerless to stop the battering ram of German energy, and were forced to fall back to defences at La Vacquerie, previously vacated by the Germans. Here the Germans were stopped, unable to make further headway against a formidable determination to hold on.

German progress in the more northerly parts of the front was even more minimal and equally costly. Around Masnières, the German 30th Division was initially unable to dislodge the 29th Division, and the German 107th Division suffered heavily while trying unsuccessfully to push British troops out of the lines around Marcoing. Fighting around Fontaine and Cantaing also inflicted heavy casualties on the Germans for little physical consequence, although the German thrusts here were largely of a diversionary nature. At Bourlon Wood, the German 3rd Guards Division pushed forward against 141st Division, confident that the British troops, horribly weakened by phosgene gas, would crumble. They didn't and put up another legendary defence.

The Germans might have had higher hopes from their most northerly line of attack, delivered via *Gruppe Arras*. This assault began later, at around 0900hrs. In the ninety minutes before boots began to move across the battlefield, the German artillery delivered a whirlwind of fire on the British lines, which brought intense counter-battery fire in return. The three German divisions – the 49th, 214th and 221st – began their push, but straight into the mouths of waiting British guns (Byng had expected a counter-attack in this part of the front and had made appropriate preparations). The British artillery blew gaping, bloody holes in the German ranks, while the British infantry also fought with passion, even launching localised counter-attacks of their own at times. Vickers machine-guns sent out tens of thousands of rounds across the countryside, which for the German attackers was unmercifully open on this part of the front. Brigadier General Edward Coke of the 169th Brigade later wrote of the chaos and courage:

> From the bank just above my little battle headquarters we had an excellent view of Bourlon Wood and the surrounding country. At 9.00 am we could see at least 3 battalions of Germans coming over the open at us, and with his field guns being brought into position by horse teams. Needless to say not a moment was lost in getting our own artillery on to them and their columns were severely cut up. However, their attack was by no means entirely stopped, and my men had a long and bitter bombing fight in the trenches – the Boches nearly turned us out, but we counter-attacked and succeeded in keeping our positions. The fight continued until about 4.00 p.m. and it was a long and anxious day for us all.
>
> Brigadier General Edward Coke, letter to Lieutenant General Thomas Snow, 6 December 1917

Night eventually drew itself over the frontline. The strategic picture was mixed, depending on perspective. The German onslaught had undoubtedly dealt the British a stunning blow. As much as we can emphasise the British resilience in defence, there was also chaos and defeat in the day, particularly in the south of the front, and many of the German divisions ended the day having made advances. Furthermore, the German counter-attack was an emphatic nail in the coffin of British ambitions at Cambrai. The sheer strength of the German response meant that any future in-depth exploitation was impossible, although this lesson had already been learnt by many at this point.

However, nor was the full picture weighted in favour of the Germans. The attack had been launched with brio, crushing artillery resources and innovative tactics – much like the British attack ten days earlier – but unlike the British assault the gains were unimpressive and the cost great. Yet this was just the beginning of both the German counter-attack and the British response.

Von Ludendorff fully intended to keep up the pressure, in the hope of a British collapse. Although *Gruppe Arras* had largely stalled around Fontaine and Cantaing, in the south the Germans aimed to keep attacking on the Masnières to Gouzeaucourt front against III Corps. Yet as the first day of December dawned, von der Marwitz came in for an unpleasant surprise when Byng launched his own dawn pre-emptive counter-attack. The Guards Division was given the task of capturing Gauche Wood and Gonnelieu, with the 5th Cavalry Division in support, while elements of the 4th Cavalry Division assaulted towards Villers-Guisland. In total, thirty-nine tanks would accompany the strike.

The British counter-attack was not destined to rearrange the battle lines in any profound way, but it certainly had a spoiling effect on the German counter-attack. The 5th Cavalry and the Guards were successful at Gauche Wood, taking the German positions there. At Gonnelieu, the Guards Division and twenty tanks became locked in a brutal clash with several German battalions that were themselves moving into the attack. The

British troops were forced back to the edge of the village, but the German attack in that sector was effectively stalled. An attempt by the 2nd Lancers to take Villers-Guislan was redolent of a previous age of warfare. The lancers attacked in traditional cavalry style, the German defenders shocked to see mounted troops rushing towards them with lances at the ready. One of the lancers later painted an evocative and proud picture of the assault:

> This was the first time we have been called upon to fight as cavalry in our three years' field service. Our regiment was in the forefront of the attack, and [so was] my squadron. Thanks be to God, the attack was made with the utmost bravery and it achieved splendid results. The fury of our charge and the ardour of our war cries so alarmed the enemy that he left his trenches and fled. At first we were assailed by machine-gun fire like a rainstorm from left and right, and afterwards from the front, but how could the cowardly Germans stand before onslaught of the braves of Khalsa?!
>
> Jiwan Singh, letter, 10 December 1917

Despite some spirited horsemanship, the cavalry's attack was stopped by barbed wire and the gathering storm of small-arms and machine-gun fire. Many of the cavalry troops were first forced to dismount, then to retreat to safer positions, incurring heavy casualties amongst horses and men. Nevertheless, the 2nd Lancers continued to be aggressive towards the Germans throughout the day.

Gruppe Busigny was unable to gather any real momentum across the whole front on 1 December, although the fighting was certainly appalling, particularly at La Vacquerie, Les Rues Vertes, Masnières and on the St Quentin canal. The force of the German push gathered most strength at La Vacquerie, with eyewitnesses noting how the British trenches there were choked with the dead and wounded of the Guards, 12th and 20th Divisions. These embattled troops were eventually relieved later in the day by the

61st Division, who would continue to hold out in positions on the outskirts of the village for the next few days.

The power of the German thrust at Masnières was eventually more than the British troops there could withstand, and they pulled back from the village. At the St Quentin canal there were ferocious close-quarter trench battles, in which German and British troops, separated by no more than a trench section, slugged it out with grenades, pistols and other hand-held weapons, all under the constant harrying artillery fire. The effects of this shellfire on fragile human forms could be appalling, as Captain James Neville of the 2nd Oxfordshire and Buckinghamshire Light Infantry described:

> As soon as it got dark, we collected some bits of men, put them in a sandbag, carried out the recognisable bodies over the top and dumped them in a shell hole, and Billy Barnard said the Lord's Prayer over the remains. I think it was probably the only prayer he knew for certain.
>
> Captain J. Neville, *The War Letters of a Light Infantryman*
> (London, Sifton Praed, 1930), p.75

The British also experienced the depredations of large numbers of German ground-attack aircraft, which swarmed over the front lines to deliver bombs and strafing runs. Naturally, the RFC threw up all its fighters in response, resulting in a vast aerial dogfight over many sectors. When the opportunities presented themselves, the British aviators also delivered ground-attack missions, as Lieutenant Arthur Gould Lee, 46 Squadron, RFC, remembered:

> I found a large body of infantry moving in mass along the very road which, ten mornings ago, Charles and I had led 'C' Flight in the bombing of Lanteau Wood. I flew along the column at 100 feet and released a bomb. The explosion jerked up my tail. With a target like this, from so low a height, I couldn't miss. It was appalling to look back as I swerved away, and see what I can

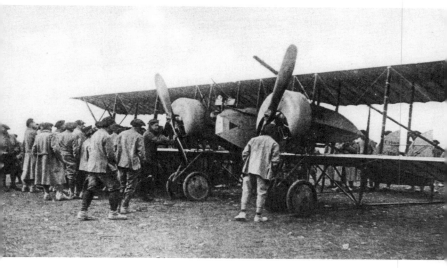

50. *The evolution in aeroplane technology was continual throughout the Great War, as the RFC played an increasingly important role in Allied operations. Here a new double-engined biplane with central gun is being inspected. The Illustrated War News, 31 May 1916.*

only describe as a hole that the bomb had made in a crowd of human beings. Next, I saw a Camel diving. It was Robinson, who had found a big group of guns lining a hedge, and after making sure that they were Boche, I joined him, got rid of my remaining bombs as well as some long bursts with my gun. Between us we put those batteries out of business for some time.

Arthur Gould Lee, *No Parachute: A Fighter Pilot in The First World War* (London, The Adventurers Club, 1969), pp.185–6

For all the frustrations and failures of the fighting on the ground, the Battle of Cambrai was certainly proving the value and potential of air power as an ancillary to a land campaign. The lessons derived would go on to inform the post-war development of aviation as an ascendant combat arm, particularly amongst the *Luftwaffe* in the 1930s.

Exhaustion

2 December

0530hrs Germans launch a localised attack against La Vacquerie, but it is repelled. Further attacks against Marcoing and against positions south of Moeuvres are repelled

3 December

Haig confirms that the British offensive campaign is over, and that the Third Army will retreat to the Flesquières Ridge Line. The German high command also plans to settle into fixed positions for the winter

4–7 Dec

The British forces perform a staged withdrawal back to the Flesquières Ridge Line. The Battle of Cambrai is over

After 1 December 1917, the Battle of Cambrai began a slow and inevitable wind-down, as both sides exhausted themselves in continual onslaughts against enemy lines and positions, and battled with the winter weather. Crucially, Byng – seeing the writing on the wall – had been directing much effort into preparing strong British defensive lines along and behind the existing frontline, wrapping around Flesquières and Ribécourt and running down between Gouzeaucourt and Gonnelieu. The Third Army could fall back to the 'Flesquières Ridge Line' and hold out for the winter. Across the lines, von der Marwitz and Rupprecht were also coming to the same conclusion, and looked to consolidate as much territory as possible before the winter locked the two sides fast in the landscape.

The decrease in the fighting would not have been immediately apparent, as combat continued intensively on 2 December. German forces continued to hammer at the Gloucesters holding on at La Vacquerie, despite the fact that the day was meant to be one of recuperation, in preparation for a more powerful co-ordinated attack on La Vacquerie and Trescault on 3 December.

51. *Captured German field guns waiting to be removed by British troops, near Ribécourt. The Illustrated London News, 1 December 1917.*

The intensity of the German artillery fire and infantry assaults began to make some progress, and by the end of the day the British defenders had been pushed to the southern and eastern perimeter of the village. German assaults at Marcoing and near Moeuvres, however, came to nothing.

The next day was a crucial one in the final chapters of the Battle of Cambrai. In the upper levels of the British command, Haig made clear that he had had enough, and sent a telegram to the War Cabinet in London admitting that further prosecution of the offensive, and indeed holding the existing positions, was strategically unwise:

> The present line could be held, but in view of the enemy's present activity it would use up troops which, in view of your instructions and the manpower situation, I do not feel justified in devoting to it. My available reserves to meet serious attack are very limited; and the troops need as much rest as possible after their strenuous exertions since April.
>
> Sir Douglas Haig, 3 December 1917

The overshadowing fact in British minds was that Germany was almost certainly preparing a major offensive on the Western Front for 1918, given that Russia's recent withdrawal from the war had released numerous German divisions from service on the Eastern Front. Britain needed to conserve its manpower, and a prolonged battle of attrition around Cambrai would serve little purpose except to pour more blood into the ground. By the time the Germans launched their counter-stroke on 30 November, III and IV Corps had already lost 19,780 men dead, wounded and missing. On the day of the counter-attack itself, another 6,000 British troops were taken prisoner. There was only one choice for Haig and Byng – a strategic withdrawal.

So it was, between 4 and 7 December, that the Third Army moved back in stages to the Flesquières Ridge Line, crossing through a landscape littered with bodies, abandoned and destroyed artillery pieces, wrecked tanks and the general detritus of war. Despite the beating the British forces had taken, the retreat was performed in an exemplary fashion. Using rear-guard forces to hold off the constant German pressure, the British troops were able to fall back in good order. They left behind them places that had been astonishing sites of effort and bloodshed – Bourlon Wood, Cantaing, the St Quentin canal, Marcoing, La Vacquerie and others. The Germans squeezed forward as the British retreated, also passing through landscapes that had cost them dear. By 8 December, however, the British were ensconced on the Flesquières Ridge Line and the Germans were also settling into their new trenches. Apart from the interminable low-level rattle of war that continued for months to come, the Battle of Cambrai was over.

AFTER THE BATTLE

As the Cambrai front fell into (relative) quiet, it was time for both sides to assess what they had achieved, and to draw appropriate lessons. The final butcher's bill for the British from 20 November to 7 December was about 45,000 casualties, with nearly half of that figure being fatalities or missing. The Germans had suffered casualties on a similar scale.

For the British, both the public and the military command, Cambrai had gone from being a eulogised victory to a public embarrassment. How, it was asked, could a campaign that secured such decisive advances on the opening day, almost unprecedented in the war to date, thereafter unwind into attrition and withdrawal? At its high point, the British advance took it to the northern extremity of Bourlon Wood, 4 miles from the original jumping off point, the Hindenburg Line having been breached and the British troops penetrating the rearmost Siegfried II Line. Bourlon Wood, plus its neighbouring village and places such as Fontaine, Cantaing, Graincourt, Noyelles, Marcoing and Masnières had seen epic battles, and the sacrifice of tens of thousands of men. Yet all of these locations were eventually abandoned during the 6,000yd retreat back to the Flesquières Ridge Line. The British had still made distinct gains when their final position was compared to the original front lines, but the 2-mile final advance was poor comfort to planners

52. Despite the apparent success, both sides still felt the pain of heavy casualties after Cambrai. The Illustrated London News, 1 December 1917.

who had originally envisioned taking Cambrai – now well behind German lines – and of making a fast cavalry advance deep into the enemy rear, possibly changing the fortunes of the entire Western Front campaign in the process. In addition, for a time during those first few days of fighting, it seemed that the British had indeed hit upon a new way of fighting that might signal an end to the bad old days of mass death for mere yards of gain, such as happened at the Somme and Ypres. Instead, the battle devolved into a familiar picture of trench-bound troops and stasis. What had gone wrong?

Investigation

Even as the battle-weary British troops, or their relief, settled into the Flesquières Ridge Line for the winter, the fire of disappointment in Britain was growing in heat and light. The War Cabinet wanted to find blame where it lay, and so ordered an official inquiry to be launched, headed by General Jan Smuts. Haig, Byng and others were now in the spotlight, and it was evidently not going to be a delicate study of failure.

53. Villagers are evacuated from Noyelles, escaping the heavy German machine-gun fire. The Illustrated London News, 1 December 1917.

One of the key questions of the inquiry was why the British had seemed so surprised by the powerful German counter-attack on 30 November. Indeed, intelligence suggested that the Germans had built up their manpower and artillery to levels that indicated an imminent push back, but there was a prevailing belief that the British offensive had exhausted the enemy and that he was in no fit state to deliver a coherent and major retaliation. Testimony from the GOC of the 12th Division, Major General A.B. Scott, for example, revealed that reports had reached divisional headquarters of preparatory activity going on behind enemy lines, but that these reports were classified as what Robert Woollcombe terms 'trench gossip'.

Another question the inquiry attempted to answer was why there had been such a significant collapse of the III Corps and VII Corps troops on the right flank of the Cambrai front, despite the German attack in these areas being the weakest of the three prongs of advance. There were alarming tales of entire units dropping their weapons and simply sprinting for the rear, although as the narrative above has shown, there was plenty of determined resistance on 30 November as well. Furthermore, reinforcements and easily accessible reserves were not available to the frontline units, meaning that the brigade and divisional commanders were unable to stem the tide in some sectors.

The debate about the collapse of the British defence took an unpalatable turn during the proceedings, centred around the figure of General Byng. Leaving the staff and higher commanders relatively blameless, Byng focused instead on the quality and preparedness of the lower ranks. He judged that the British troops in this sector were of adequate strength, but that a lack of training accounted for their poor showing. Furthermore, he argued that the Machine Gun Corps had not exhibited 'staunchness' and that, had the troops been of sufficient quality, the German breakthrough would not have occurred.

This explanation was accepted by many within the British media, government and military. Ironically, it was Haig himself who came to the defence of the lower ranks. Popular representations of Haig tend to portray him as an imperious figure, distant from the mud-drenched concerns of the man at the frontline. His explanation for the failure to predict and stop the counter-attack, however, has a rather humble humanity:

> Whatever view may be held on the foregoing [the criticisms of the lower ranks], I feel, after careful consideration that all blame for the mishap … must rest on my shoulders. It was I who decided on the 22nd that Bourlon Wood should be attacked … The occupation of this position at once increased our front and threw extra work on our troops. As events on the 30th show, many of the men were very tired and unable to resist the enemy's blow, as I believe they could have done had they been fresher.
>
> National Archives, WO 158/52

In this passage, Haig acknowledges that all men have limits to what they can be expected to achieve, and that many of his troops had reached those limits. Furthermore, there is an implicit recognition of strategic mistakes. Byng himself had been concerned about Bourlon Wood as an early objective of the campaign, and in many ways it does appear to be a 'bridge too far'. Haig also went on to acknowledge that in certain sectors the British troops were simply faced with an enemy numerically too strong to resist, and that the rearward flow of retreating infantry probably prevented the British machine-gunners from gaining a clear line of fire on their enemy.

Despite this reappraisal, the investigations of late 1917 and early 1918 still largely put the responsibility for the collapse, if not the blame, at the door of those on the frontline. It would remain until the late 1940s for something better approaching the truth to emerge, in the form of the *Official History* of the Cambrai campaign. Detailed research showed that there had been a singular failure amongst the British senior commanders to take the possibility of a German counter-attack seriously, despite the fact that previous experience and current intelligence suggested such an attack was a virtual certainty. Exhausted and understrength battalions were therefore kept in the line when they should have been relieved or reinforced. The British commanders should have made ready for a defence, but chose not to do so. Also, the German ability to reinforce a threatened sector heavily and quickly was known to the British staff, hence the initial decision to limit the offensive to a forty-eight-hour period of action. Haig's decision to keep the campaign going forward after 21 November is therefore open to question; any extension of the offensive was likely to turn a fast strike into a prolonged grinding match.

In balance to the rationalisations of British collapse, however, is the fact that the German counter-attack failed in many of its objectives, not least the aim to restore the original Hindenburg Line defences. Indeed, von Ludendorff, Rupprecht and von der Marwitz also spent much time reflecting on what had gone wrong with the German plan. The conclusions included a counter-attack over too wide a front, diffusing any decisive punch. Furthermore, like the British soldiers facing them, many troops of the German Second Army were also on their last legs, exhausted even before they attempted to turn the tide. Lastly, however, the post-mortem acknowledged that the British defence had been of unexpected tenacity, inflicting high levels of casualties and proving difficult to shift. So much for a lack of British 'staunchness'.

SHELL SHOCK

The British forces suffered more than 80,000 shell shock victims during the First World War. The term 'shell shock' referred to the belief that what we now classify as the symptoms of post-traumatic stress disorder (PTSD) were actually caused by the physiological effect of artillery shell detonations on the human brain.

Seeing the Future

Such were the official strategic diagnoses of the Battle of Cambrai. On a tactical level, the lessons that emerge from the campaign are important in the history of warfare. We see at Cambrai both the success and failure of innovation, on both the British and the German sides, hence the campaign has been combed over ever since by military analysts.

More than any other factor, it has been the role of the tank that has attracted the lion's share of analysis of Cambrai, and there is much to credit this focus. At Cambrai, tanks were used in numbers that had never been seen before on a battlefield, and with a wholesale tactical co-ordination with artillery and infantry. Here was true integration of weapons systems and human beings in combined-arms warfare, the concept of which would become the hallmark of almost all subsequent war fighting. Certainly, there is no denying that the tanks were a key ingredient in the successes of 20–21 November. Following a short, stunning artillery barrage, the tanks were able to close on the German trenches, largely with impunity to small-arms fire, then deliver close-range cannon and machine-gun fire directly into the German positions, all from a mobile platform. Many Germans surrendered just from shock alone. That the tanks were also able to scour a path through the German barbed wire, overcoming one of the central problems of trench assaults since 1915, was a seminal advance.

As the battle wore on, and the shock of armour on the German defenders wore off, the authority of the tank became more open to question. Cambrai provided the lesson, still relevant to the mighty main battle tanks of today, that a tank fighting isolated from infantry is virtually inviting destruction. In the contested villages of the Cambrai battle front, dozens of tanks were destroyed while roaming and fighting alone in narrow streets. Death might come from field guns or machine-guns firing armour-piercing ammunition, but also from tank-hunting teams of *Stoßtruppen*. In Fontaine on 23 November, for example, soldiers hunted tanks at close quarters while armed with sandbags filled with hand grenades, the handle and fuse of one of the grenades tied jutting out from the neck of the bag. The soldiers would simply close on one of the tanks unseen from its 'blind' approaches (over rough terrain the soldiers could often run or even walk as fast as the tank could drive), pull the fuse cord on the exposed grenade and throw the bag under a

54. *Tanks often found it difficult and dangerous to manouevre through narrow village streets. The Illustrated London News, 1 December 1917.*

track. The detonation of the four grenades together would blow off a track, resulting in what is called a 'disability kill'. For such reasons, one lesson of Cambrai was that however impressive the armoured vehicle, it must work in unison with surrounding infantry, who could protect the tank from just such attacks.

Enemy action was not the only thing to limit the usefulness of the tank. Tree stumps could wreck a track or the underneath of a hull. A wide trench could trap some tanks within it, if they had not the means to either cross the trench (a fascine) or pull themselves free. Mechanical failures were constant, resulting in tanks being abandoned in zones not conducive to safe repairs or recovery. The environment inside the tanks, explained above, also limited the ability of the crew to negotiate the terrain and spot tactical opportunities.

Most of the tanks that started the Cambrai battle would not see the end of it. However, while many infantry came to have a sceptical view of the new armour, some also recognised that, used judiciously, they could have a real benefit:

> We had, or some of us had, lost faith in the tanks. Those abandoned hulks scattered in front of Cambrai proved to some that their usefulness was limited. Those big bundles of tree loppings carried on top ready for dropping into an otherwise impassable trench demonstrated their limitations. And some said, what was wrong with some of the hulks we had seen (and closely examined) lying around abandoned? Some with not a visible scratch or a sign of serious damage, but left there as sitting targets for enemy field guns. But we who had been in Bourlon village knew that one tank at the right time at the right place could have avoided the slaughter of two or three hundred men on that damp, chilly morning of November 26th 1917.
>
> F. Wynne, IWM doc 9750

Here infantry corporal Fred Wynne, 13th East Surreys, expressed the mix of derision and respect the tanks attracted. Perhaps the greatest lesson of Cambrai was that armour had to be consistently and continuously used as part of an integrated armour/artillery/infantry package, preferably on suitable terrain, if it was to make its mark on the battlefield.

One further interesting point to come out of the post-battle analysis was that of over-commitment in the early stages of the clash. Various reports pointed to the fact that vast quantities of manpower and armour were thrown against the immediate Hindenburg Line objectives, which were easily cracked. The upshot of this focus, however, was that the weaker follow-on forces had mission goals greater than they could achieve. The battle front was also a short one; hence the density of men thrown into the attack meant that the offensive's major reserve force – V Corps – had to be held much farther away, in fact nearly 20 miles behind the frontline.

Still focusing on the problems of exploitation, we see that the British cavalry failed to find their moment to shine. In many

55. Cavalry slowly wend their way over a reserve line road in territory just captured from the Germans. The Illustrated London News, 1 December 1917.

ways, the Cavalry Corps was hobbled from the start. Its battalions were drawn up in assembly areas set well behind the front of action, so time was lost to bring the cavalry forward into action. Communications were slow and problematic (for everyone, not just for cavalry), which also meant that the cavalry units had absent or impartial orders at critical moments in the battle. For all these restrictions, there was no denying that the cavalry as an arm of service had issues with its very tactical identity. Although there were hoof-thundering mounted strikes at particular moments on the battlefield, barbed wire, machine-guns and artillery ensured that men on horses could not act as a means of decision during the action. Had they actually attempted to make a deep penetration into the German-held territory, they would have fallen beyond the range of artillery and infantry support, and would likely have come to a sticky end.

The Germans also took stock of the Battle of Cambrai and studied its lessons. One of the most shocking aspects of the initial German defeat was how the British had managed to overload the 'elastic defence' in which the Germans had so much confidence. In a similar style to the German *Blitzkrieg* of 1939–40, the British delivered a concentrated combined-arms punch that crashed through several lines of defences. *Eingreifentaktik* had eventually come into play, but much later and much farther back than planned.

Cambrai also taught the Germans a salutary lesson about defensive warfare. The fact was that the Hindenburg Line defences were some of the best of the entire war, constructed at reasonable leisure while the fighting continued further out to the west. It was clear that static defences, no matter how convincing, were now under threat from the developments in armour and artillery, particularly the former. Mobility was beginning to take precedence on the modern battlefield, and simply remaining in trench positions invited being outmanoeuvred and shelled into destruction. Rupprecht memorably noted: 'Wherever the ground offers suitable going for tanks, surprise attacks like this may be expected. That being the case, there can be no more mention, therefore, of quiet fronts.'

The German forces nevertheless took some positive lessons from the Battle of Cambrai. Like the British, they had proved the value of combat aviation acting as flying fire support. The aircraft of the *Luftstreitkräfte* did not possess the bomb technology to deliver the earth-battering destruction seen in the Second World War, but they did inflict both casualties and tactical limitations on individual British units.

In time, aircraft would also become one of the greatest scourges of armour. Yet Cambrai has also revealed that the Germans were quite capable of dealing with tanks, once they had psychologically risen to the challenge. Although specific anti-tank technologies were seriously lacking, a confident field-gun crew with armour-piercing ammunition was a serious problem to a Mk IV tank, particularly in terrain favourable to ambush. Infantry assault teams also learnt the same lesson, and soon observed that you didn't need to destroy a tank entirely to render it combat ineffective.

Finally, the German counter-attack on 30 November also proved the value of *Stoßtruppen* tactics. Again, mobility was the keyword here, using manoeuvrability and speed, plus lots of transportable firepower, to overwhelm the enemy at key points or to bypass strongpoints and leave them for heavier follow-on forces. These tactics were tested in their fullest the following year, during the spring offensives that for a time threatened total defeat for the Allies (see next chapter). Taken together, Cambrai was a testing ground for new ways of war. In many ways, the sun was now setting over the age of trench warfare.

THE LEGACY

Cambrai showed that the German Army was still a force to be reckoned with, and events of spring 1918 left the Allies in no doubt. On 21 March, the German Army launched the massive *Kaiserschlacht* (Kaiser's Battle) offensive across much of the Western Front, utilising every innovation in artillery, infantry tactics and air power. The strength of the attack was overwhelming; German divisions released from the Eastern Front meant that Germany even enjoyed numerical superiority. The British Fifth Army began a precipitate collapse, losing 55,000 troops in the first day.

What occurred between March and July 1918 was one of the Allies' greatest tactical defeats of the war. Unlike many previous battles, here was an action of serious long-range movement – by the end of the May, British and French forces were even pressed back against the River Marne, where they had fought to save Paris in 1914. For a time, it seemed as if four years of Allied bloodshed had been in vain.

Events were to prove otherwise. The *Kaiserschlacht* was truly the last gasp of Imperial Germany. Stretched logistics, irreplaceable casualties and sheer exhaustion had run the German advance into the ground. Furthermore, the Allies were now enjoying the inexorable build-up of men and materiel provided by the entry of the United States into the war. During June and July, German

56. After Cambrai, the British government were keen to extol the virtues of the tank to the public. Here, one of the tanks used in the Cambrai battle is placed in Trafalgar Square as a 'tank bank', encouraging visitors to purchase a 'tank bond' or 'tank certificate' to help raise funds to manufacture more of these 'iron monsters'. The Illustrated London News, 1 December 1917.

offensives petered out into local withdrawals, then in August the Allies recovered themselves and launched their own major counter-offensive.

Now the once defiant German Army began to fold. During the Battle of Amiens alone (8–11 August), the German Army took losses of 74,000 men, including 50,000 captured. In September

57. British tank at Cambrai, bringing in a captured German artillery piece. War of the Nations, New York Times Co., New York, 1919. Courtesy of www.gwpda.org.uk

German troops were back on the Hindenburg Line, where they had begun their offensive six months earlier. In October, the collapse increased in pace, with successive trench systems being overrun. The end was inevitable.

On 11 November 1918, Germany signed the Armistice with the Allies, accepting its final defeat in the First World War. The war had taken some 17 million lives, for reasons that are hard to fathom from today's less imperial age. Taken in this context, Cambrai was a relatively small clash, a localised and fairly short battle that decided little in terms of the overall strategy of the war. Yet as we have acknowledged, the battle sowed early seeds of future warfare. In the inter-war years, the principles and practices of combined-arms, armour-led combat would be refined and practised. Ironically, it would be the Germans who would eventually lead the way in armoured warfare. The *Blitzkrieg* they unleashed from September 1939 brought them conquests unimaginable in the First World War – by the end of 1941, virtually all of Western Europe, the Balkans, Poland and much of the western Soviet Union would be under German occupation. Panzers were at the forefront of all these conquests, used effectively in combination with increasingly mechanised infantry, ground-attack aircraft and anti-tank support units, all co-ordinated using radio communications. The Battle of Cambrai provided glimpses of this dark future, as well as being a battle of singular drama in its own right.

ORDERS OF BATTLE

British Third Army (Gen. Hon. Sir J.H.G. Byng)

III Corps (Lt Gen. Sir W.P. Pulteney)

6th Division (Maj. Gen. T.O. Marden)
16th Infantry Brigade (Brig. Gen. H.A. Walker)
      1st Battalion King's Shropshire Light Infantry
      1st Battalion East Kent Regiment 'Buffs'
      2nd Battalion York and Lancaster Regiment
      8th Battalion Bedfordshire Regiment
18th Infantry Brigade (Brig. Gen. G.S.G. Craufurd)
      1st Battalion West Yorkshire Regiment
      2nd Battalion Durham Light Infantry
      11th Battalion Essex Regiment (attached to 71st Brigade
      for Operation GY)
      14th Battalion Durham Light Infantry
71st Infantry Brigade (Brig. Gen. P.W. Brown)
      1st Battalion Leicestershire Regiment
      2nd Battalion Sherwood Foresters
      9th Battalion Suffolk Regiment
      9th Battalion Norfolk Regiment

20th (Light) Division (Maj. Gen. H.H.G. Douglas Smith)
59th Infantry Brigade (Brig. Gen. H.H.G. Hyslop)
- 10th Battalion Rifle Brigade
- 11th Battalion Rifle Brigade
- 10th Battalion King's Royal Rifle Corps
- 11th Battalion King's Royal Rifle Corps

60th Infantry Brigade (Brig. Gen. F.J. Duncan)
- 6th Battalion Oxfordshire and Buckinghamshire Light Infantry
- 6th Battalion King's Shropshire Light Infantry
- 12th Battalion Rifle Brigade
- 12th Battalion King's Royal Rifle Corps

61st Infantry Brigade (Brig. Gen. W.E. Banbury)
- 7th Battalion Duke of Cornwall's Light Infantry
- 7th Battalion Somerset Light Infantry
- 7th Battalion King's Own Yorkshire Light Infantry
- 12th Battalion Liverpool Regiment (King's)

12th (Eastern) Division (Maj. Gen. A.B. Scott)
35th Infantry Brigade (Brig. Gen. B. Vincent)
- 5th Battalion Royal Berkshire Regiment
- 7th Battalion Suffolk Regiment
- 7th Battalion Norfolk Regiment
- 9th Battalion Essex Regiment

36th Infantry Brigade (Brig. Gen. C.S. Owen)
- 7th Battalion Sussex Regiment
- 8th Battalion Royal Fusiliers (City of London)
- 9th Battalion Royal Fusiliers (City of London)
- 11th Battalion Middlesex Regiment

37th Infantry Brigade (Brig. Gen. Incledon-Weber)
- 6th Battalion East Kent Regiment 'Buffs'
- 6th Battalion Royal West Kent Regiment (Queen's Own)
- 6th Battalion West Surrey Regiment (Queen's Own)
- 7th Battalion East Surrey Regiment

29th Division (Maj. Gen. Sir H. de Beauvoir de Lisle)
86th Infantry Brigade (Brig. Gen. G.R.H. Cheape)
        1st Battalion Royal Guernsey Light Infantry
        1st Battalion Lancashire Fusiliers
        2nd Battalion Royal Fusiliers (City of London)
        16th Battalion Middlesex Regiment
87th Infantry Brigade (Brig. Gen. C.H.T. Lucas)
        1st Battalion King's Own Borders
        1st Battalion Border Regiment
        1st Battalion Lancashire Fusiliers
        2nd Battalion South Wales Borderers
88th Infantry Brigade (Brig. Gen. H. Nelson)
        1st Battalion Essex Regiment
        1st Battalion Newfoundland Regiment
        2nd Battalion Hampshire Regiment
        4th Battalion Worcestershire Regiment

IV Corps (Lt Gen. Sir C.L. Woollcombe)

36th (Ulster) Division (Maj. Gen. O.S.W. Nugent)
107th Infantry Brigade (Brig. Gen. W.N. Withycombe)
        1st Battalion Royal Irish Fusiliers
        6th Battalion Royal Irish Rifles
        9th Battalion Royal Irish Rifles
        10th Battalion Royal Irish Rifles
108th Infantry Brigade (Brig. Gen. C.R.J. Griffith)
        9th Battalion Royal Irish Fusiliers
        11th Battalion Royal Irish Rifles
        12th Battalion Royal Irish Rifles
        13th Battalion Royal Irish Rifles
109th Infantry Brigade (Brig. Gen. A. St Q. Ricardo)
        9th Battalion Royal Inniskilling Fusiliers
        10th Battalion Royal Inniskilling Fusiliers
        11th Battalion Royal Inniskilling Fusiliers
        14th Battalion Royal Irish Rifles

Orders of Battle

51st (Highland) Division (Maj. Gen. G.M. Harper)
152nd Infantry Brigade (Brig. Gen. H.P. Burn)
     5th Battalion Seaforth Highlanders
     6th Battalion Seaforth Highlanders
     6th Battalion Gordon Highlanders
     8th Battalion Argyll and Sutherland Highlanders
153rd Infantry Brigade (Brig. Gen. A.T. Beckwith)
     5th Battalion Gordon Highlanders
     7th Battalion Gordon Highlanders
     6th Battalion Black Watch
     7th Battalion Black Watch
154th Infantry Brigade (Brig. Gen. K.G. Buchanan)
     4th Battalion Gordon Highlanders
     4th Battalion Seaforth Highlanders
     7th Battalion Argyll and Sutherland Highlanders
     9th Battalion Royal Scots

62nd (West Riding) Division (Maj. Gen. Sir W.P. Braithwaite)
185th Infantry Brigade (Brig. Gen. Viscount Hampden)
     5th Battalion West Yorkshire Regiment
     6th Battalion West Yorkshire Regiment
     7th Battalion West Yorkshire Regiment
     8th Battalion West Yorkshire Regiment
186th Infantry Brigade (Brig. Gen. R.B. Bradford VC)
     4th Battalion Duke of Wellington's Regiment
     5th Battalion Duke of Wellington's Regiment
     6th Battalion Duke of Wellington's Regiment
     7th Battalion Duke of Wellington's Regiment
187th Infantry Brigade (Brig. Gen. R. O'B. Taylor)
     4th Battalion King's Own Yorkshire Light Infantry
     5th Battalion King's Own Yorkshire Light Infantry
     4th Battalion York and Lancaster Regiment
     5th Battalion York and Lancaster Regiment

Tank Corps (Brig. Gen. H.J. Elles)

I Tank Brigade (Col C. D'A. Baker Carr)
   'D' Battalion Tank Corps
   'E' Battalion Tank Corps
   'G' Battalion Tank Corps
II Tank Brigade (Col A. Courage)
   'A' Battalion Tank Corps
   'B' Battalion Tank Corps
   'H' Battalion Tank Corps
III Tank Brigade (Col J. Hardress-Lloyd)
   'C' Battalion Tank Corps
   'F' Battalion Tank Corps
   'I' Battalion Tank Corps

Cavalry Corps (Lt Gen. C.T. McM. Kavanagh)

1st Cavalry Division (Maj. Gen. R.L. Mullens)
1st Cavalry Brigade (Brig. Gen. E. Makins)
   2nd Dragoon Guards (Queen's Bays)
   5th Dragoon Guards (Princess Charlotte of Wales)
   11th Hussars (Prince Albert's Own)
2nd Cavalry Brigade (Brig. Gen. D.J.E. Beale-Brown)
   4th Dragoon Guards (Royal Irish)
   9th Lancers (Queen's Royal)
   18th Hussars (Queen Mary's Own)
9th Cavalry Brigade (Brig. Gen. D'A. Legard)
   1st Bedfordshire Yeomanry
   15th Hussars (The King's)
   19th Hussars (Queen Alexandra's Own Royal)

2nd Cavalry Division (Maj. Gen. W.H. Greenly)
3rd Cavalry Brigade (n/k)
   4th Hussars (Queen's Own)

5th Lancers (Royal Irish)
4th Cavalry Brigade (n/k)
6th Dragoon Guards (Carabiniers)
3rd Hussars (King's Own)
1st Oxfordshire Yeomanry
5th Cavalry Brigade (Brig. Gen. C.L.K. Campbell)
2nd Dragoons (Royal Scots Greys)
12th Lancers (Prince of Wales' Own Royal)
20th Hussars

3rd Cavalry Division (Brig. Gen. A.E.W. Harman)
6th Cavalry Brigade (n/k)
1st Royal Dragoons
1st North Somerset Yeomanry
3rd Dragoon Guards (Prince of Wales')
7th Cavalry Brigade (n/k)
1st Life Guards
2nd Life Guards
Royal Horse Guards
8th Cavalry Brigade (n/k)
10th Hussars (Prince of Wales' Own Royal)
1st Essex Yeomanry

4th Cavalry Division (Maj. Gen. A.A. Kennedy)
Sialkot Cavalry Brigade (n/k)
17th Lancers (Duke of Cambridge's Own)
6th Cavalry (King Edward's Own)
19th Lancers (Fane's Horse)
Mhow Cavalry Brigade (Brig. Gen. N.M. Haig)
2nd Lancers (Gardner's Horse)
6th Inniskilling Dragoons
38th Central India Horse (King George's Own)
Lucknow Cavalry Brigade (Brig. Gen. M.F. Gage)
29th Lancers (Deccan Horse)

36th Jacob's Horse
Jodhpur Lancers

5th Cavalry Division (Maj. Gen. H.J.M. MacAndrew)
Ambala Cavalry Brigade (Brig. Gen. C.H. Rankin)
    8th Hussars (King's Royal Irish)
    9th Lancers (Hodson's Horse)
    18th Lancers (King George's Own)
Secunderabad Cavalry Brigade (n/k)
    7th Dragoon Guards (Princess Royal's)
    34th Poona Horse
    20th Lancers (Deccan Horse)
Canadian Cavalry Brigade (Brig. Gen. J.E.B. Seely)
    Lord Strathcona's Horse
    Fort Garry Horse
    Royal Canadian Dragoons

Units deployed into the battle from 23 November:

Guards Division (Maj. Gen. G.P.T. Feilding)
1st Guards Brigade (Brig. Gen. C.R. Champion de Crespigny)
    1st Battalion Irish Guards
    2nd Battalion Grenadier Guards
    2nd Battalion Coldstream Guards
    3rd Battalion Coldstream Guards
2nd Guards Brigade (Brig. Gen. B.N. Sergison Brooke)
    1st Battalion Coldstream Guards
    1st Battalion Scots Guards
    2nd Battalion Irish Guards
    3rd Battalion Grenadier Guards
3rd Guards Brigade (Brig. Gen. Lord Seymour)
    1st Battalion Grenadier Guards
    1st Battalion Welsh Guards
    2nd Battalion Scots Guards
    4th Battalion Grenadier Guards

Orders of Battle

40th Division (Maj. Gen. J. Ponsonby)

119th Infantry Brigade (Brig. Gen. F.P. Crozier)

    19th Battalion Royal Welch Fusiliers

    12th Battalion South Wales Borderers

    17th Battalion Welsh Regiment

    18th Battalion Welsh Regiment

120th Infantry Brigade (n/k)

    13th Battalion East Surrey Regiment

    14th Battalion Highland Light Infantry

    14th Battalion Argyll and Sutherland Highlanders

    11th Battalion Royal Lancaster Regiment (King's Own)

121st Infantry Brigade (Brig. Gen. J. Campbell)

    12th Battalion Suffolk Regiment

    13th Battalion Yorkshire Regiment

    20th Battalion Middlesex Regiment

    21st Battalion Middlesex Regiment

56th (1st London) Division (Maj. Gen. F.A. Dudgeon)

167th Infantry Brigade (Brig. Gen. G.H.B. Freeth)

    1st Battalion Royal Fusiliers (City of London)

    3rd Battalion Royal Fusiliers (City of London)

    7th Battalion Middlesex Regiment

    8th Battalion Middlesex Regiment

168th Infantry Brigade (n/k)

    4th Battalion Royal Fusiliers (City of London)

    12th Battalion London Regiment (The Rangers)

    13th Battalion London Regiment (Kensington)

    14th Battalion London Regiment (London Scottish)

169th Infantry Brigade (Brig. Gen. E.S.D'E. Coke)

    2nd Battalion Royal Fusiliers (City of London)

    5th Battalion London Regiment (London Rifle Brigade)

    9th Battalion London Regiment (Queen Victoria Rifles)

    16th Battalion London Regiment (Queen's Westminster Rifles)

2nd Division (Maj. Gen. C.E. Pereira)

5th Infantry Brigade (Brig. Gen. W. Bullen Smith)

> 2nd Battalion Oxfordshire and Buckinghamshire Light Infantry
>
> 2nd Battalion Highland Light Infantry
>
> 17th Battalion Royal Fusiliers (City of London)
>
> 24th Battalion Royal Fusiliers (City of London)

6th Infantry Brigade (Brig. Gen. R.K. Walsh)

> 1st Battalion King's Regiment (Liverpool)
>
> 2nd Battalion South Staffordshire Regiment
>
> 13th Battalion Essex Regiment
>
> 17th Battalion Middlesex Regiment

99th Infantry Brigade (Brig. Gen. R.O. Kellett)

> 1st Battalion King's Royal Rifle Corps
>
> 1st Battalion Royal Berkshire Regiment
>
> 22nd Battalion Royal Fusiliers (City of London)
>
> 23rd Battalion Royal Fusiliers (City of London)

47th (2nd London) Division (Maj. Gen. G.F. Gorringe)

140th Infantry Brigade (Brig. Gen. H.P.B.L. Kennedy)

> 6th Battalion London Regiment (City of London Rifles)
>
> 7th Battalion London Regiment (City of London)
>
> 8th Battalion London Regiment (Post Office Rifles)
>
> 15th Battalion London Regiment (Civil Service Rifles)

141st Infantry Brigade (Brig. Gen. J.F. Erskine)

> 17th Battalion London Regiment (Poplar and Stepney Rifles)
>
> 18th Battalion London Regiment (London Irish Rifles)
>
> 19th Battalion London Regiment (St Pancras)
>
> 20th Battalion London Regiment (Blackheath and Woolwich)

142nd Infantry Brigade (Brig. Gen. V.T. Bailey)

> 21st Battalion London Regiment (1st Surrey Rifles)
>
> 22nd Battalion London Regiment (The Queen's)

23rd Battalion London Regiment (County of London)
24th Battalion London Regiment (The Queen's)

55th (West Lancashire) Division (Maj. Gen. H.S. Jeudwine)
164th Brigade (Brig. Gen. C.I. Stockwell)
    4th Battalion Royal Lancaster Regiment (King's Own)
    4th Battalion Royal North Lancaster Regiment
    5th Battalion Lancashire Fusiliers
    8th Battalion King's Regiment (Liverpool)
165th Infantry Brigade (Brig. Gen. L.B. Boyd Moss)
    5th Battalion King's Regiment (Liverpool)
    6th Battalion King's Regiment (Liverpool)
    7th Battalion King's Regiment (Liverpool)
    9th Battalion King's Regiment (Liverpool)
166th Infantry Brigade (Brig. Gen. F.G. Lewis)
    5th Battalion Royal Lancaster Regiment (King's Own)
    5th Battalion South Lancashire Regiment
    10th Battalion King's Regiment (Liverpool)
    5th Battalion Royal North Lancaster Regiment

German Second Army (General von der Marwitz)

XIV Corps – Gruppe Arras (Generalleutnant von Moser)

111th Infantry Division (Generalmajor von Busse)
    73rd Fusilier Regiment
    76th Infantry Regiment
    164th Infantry Regiment

240th Infantry Division (Generalmajor Müller)
    469th Infantry Regiment
    470th Infantry Regiment
    471st Infantry Regiment

20th Infantry Division (Generalmajor Wellmann)
> 77th Infantry Regiment
> 79th Infantry Regiment
> 92nd Infantry Regiment

Reinforcements for 30 November counter-attack:

3rd Guards Infantry Division (Generalmajor von Lindequist)
> Guard Fusilier Regiment
> Lehr Infantry Regiment
> 9th Grenadier Regiment

21st Reserve Infantry Division (Generalmajor Briefe)
> 80th Reserve Infantry Regiment
> 87th Reserve Infantry Regiment
> 88th Reserve Infantry Regiment

221st Infantry Division (Generalmajor von la Chevallerie)
> 41st Infantry Regiment
> 60th Reserve Infantry Regiment
> 1st Ersatz Reserve Infantry Regiment

214th Infantry Division (Generalmajor von Brauchitsch)
> 50th Infantry Regiment
> 358th Infantry Regiment
> 363rd Infantry Regiment

49th Reserve Infantry Division (Generalmajor von Unger)
> 225th Reserve Infantry Regiment
> 226th Reserve Infantry Regiment
> 228th Reserve Infantry Regiment

XIII Corps – Gruppe Caudry (Generalleutnant von Watter)

20th Landwehr Division (Generalmajor von Hanstein)
>> 384th *Landwehr* Infantry Regiment
>> 386th *Landwehr* Infantry Regiment
>> 387th *Landwehr* Infantry Regiment

54th Infantry Division (Generalmajor von Watter)
>> 84th Infantry Regiment
>> 27th Reserve Infantry Regiment
>> 90th Reserve Infantry Regiment

9th Reserve Infantry Division (Generalmajor von Hildemann)
>> 395th Infantry Regiment
>> 6th Reserve Infantry Regiment
>> 19th Reserve Infantry Regiment

183rd Infantry Division (Generalmajor von Schüssler)
>> 184th Infantry Regiment
>> 418th Infantry Regiment
>> 440th Infantry Regiment

Reinforcements for 30 November counter-attack:

107th Infantry Division (Generalmajor Havenstein)
>> 52nd Reserve Infantry Regiment
>> 227th Reserve Infantry Regiment
>> 232nd Reserve Infantry Regiment

119th Infantry Division (Generalmajor Berger)
>> 46th Infantry Regiment
>> 58th Infantry Regiment
>> 46th Reserve Infantry Regiment

28th Infantry Division (Generalmajor Langer)
> 40th Fusilier Regiment
> Lieb Grenadier Regiment
> 110th Grenadier Regiment

30th Infantry Division (Generalmajor Freiherr von der Wenge)
> 99th Infantry Regiment
> 105th Infantry Regiment
> 143rd Infantry Regiment

220th Infantry Division (Generalmajor von Bassewitz)
> 190th Infantry Regiment
> 55th Reserve Infantry Regiment
> 99th Reserve Infantry Regiment

Created for the 30 November counter-offensive:

XXIII Corps – Gruppe Busigny (Generalleutnant von Kathen)

30th Infantry Division (Generalmajor Leezman)
> 30th Infantry Regiment
> 67th Infantry Regiment
> 145th Infantry Regiment

208th Infantry Division (Generalmajor von Grodded)
> 25th Infantry Regiment
> 65th Infantry Regiment
> 185th Infantry Regiment

5th Guards Infantry Division (Generalmajor von der Often)
> 3rd Guards Regiment
> 3rd Guards Grenadier Regiment (Elizabeth)
> 20th Infantry Regiment

FURTHER READING

Books

Bryan, Cooper, *The Ironclads of Cambrai* (London, Cassell, 1967)

Gibot, Jean-Luc and Philippe Gorcynski, *Following the Tanks: Cambrai 20 November–7 December 1917* (Arras, 1999)

Gilbert, Martin, *The First World War: A Complete History* (London, Phoenix Press, 2000)

Hammond, Bryn, *Cambrai 1917: The Myth of the First Great Tank Battle* (London, Weidenfeld & Nicolson, 2008)

Holmes, Richard, *Tommy: The British Soldier on the Western Front 1914–18* (London, HarperCollins, 2004)

Horsfall, Jack and Nigel Cave, *Cambrai: Bourlon Wood* (London, Leo Cooper, 2002)

———, *Cambrai: The Right Hook* (London, Leo Cooper, 1999)

Keegan, John, *The First World War* (London, Pimlico, 1999)

McNab, Chris, *The Somme: France 1916* (Andover, Pitkin Publishing, 2010)

Miles, Wilfred, *History of the Great War – Military Operations France and Belgium 1917 – The Battle of Cambrai* (London, 1948)

Moore, William, *A Wood Called Bourlon: The Cover-Up After Cambrai 1917* (London, Leo Cooper, 1988)

Saunders, Anthony, *The Weapons of Trench Warfare 1914–18* (Stroud, Sutton Publishing, 2000)

Smithers, A.J., *Cambrai: The First Great Tank Battle 1917* (London, Leo Cooper, 1992)

Stone, Norman, *World War One: A Short History* (London, Penguin, 2008)

Strachan, Hew, *The First World War* (London, Simon & Schuster, 2003)

Turner, Alex, *Cambrai 1917: The Birth of Armoured Warfare* (Oxford, Osprey, 2007)

Wilmott, H.P., *World War I* (London, Dorling Kindersley, 2009)

Woollcombe, Robert, *The First Tank Battle: Cambrai 1917* (London, Arthur Baker, 1967)

Useful Websites

Firstworldwar.com: Major First World War website with summary of the Battle of Cambrai and links out to documents and photos: http://www.firstworldwar.com/battles/cambrai.htm

The Long, Long Trail: Extensive First World War website with detailed Cambrai page: http://www.1914-1918.net/bat21.htm

First World War Battlefields: Website providing visitor information to First World War battlefields; includes good page on Cambrai: http://www.ww1battlefields.co.uk/others/cambrai.html

The Tank of Flesquières: Website of the association created in response to the discovery of a Mk IV tank on the Cambrai battlefield in 1998: http://www.tank-cambrai.com/english/home.php

Places to Visit

Interesting locations on the Cambrai battlefield:

- Louverval Military Cemetery (including the Cambrai Memorial to the Missing) – off D930 between Bapaume and Cambrai
- Five Points Cemetery – Ypres village
- Rocquigny-Equancourt Road British Cemetery – located between the two villages of the name
- Ribécourt Road Cemetery – just outside Trescault

- 42nd Division Memorial – on the edge of Trescault, towards Havrincourt
- 62nd (West Riding) Division Memorial – Havrincourt
- Grand Ravine Cemetery – just outside Havrincourt
- Tank Memorial – just south of Flesquières on D89
- Flesquières Hill British Cemetery – just east of Flesquières
- Canadian Memorial – on D16 just before Bourlon village

The Tank Museum
Bovington
Dorset
BH20 6JG
Tel: 01929 405096
Fax: 01929 405360
Web: http://www.tankmuseum.org/home

Imperial War Museum
Lambeth Road
London SE1 6HZ
Tel: 020 7416 5320
Web: www.iwm.org.uk

National Army Museum
Royal Hospital Road
Chelsea, London SW3 4HT
Tel: 020 7730 0717
Web: www.nam.ac.uk

INDEX